More Praise for the third edition of *Repacking Your Bags*

"Richard Leider and David Shapiro know that the world is spinning faster and faster. We need to travel with lighter and lighter baggage each year. So they've repacked their book to help us repack our bags."
—**Richard Bolles, author of *What Color Is Your Parachute? 2012***

"So often in our lives we approach that 'next chapter.' Now we have an extraordinary guidebook. Required reading for all those who seek meaning and fulfillment in their lives."
—**John Hendricks, founder and Chairman, Discovery Channel and Discovery Communications**

"This book is both profound and simple, timely and timeless. It speaks from experience and to the heart. We can all learn from it and we should all read it and we should all say 'thank you' to its authors. It's that special and that essential."
—**Alan M. Webber, cofounder, *Fast Company* magazine, and author of *Rules of Thumb***

"*Repacking Your Bags* inspires all of us with its vision and is a great guidebook for the good life."
—**Frances Hesselbein, President and CEO, The Frances Hesselbein Leadership Institute, and recipient of the Presidential Medal of Freedom**

"At a time when people have the opportunity to pursue multiple careers and live in different locations over a lifetime, this book is a guide to finding more happiness, satisfaction, and purpose along the way. It can change your life—for the better!"
—**Stephan Rechtschaffen, MD, cofounder, Omega Institute, and founder, Blue Spirit Costa Rica**

"This new edition holds the key to rethinking your life and its purpose and having the courage to follow your inner compass. It could transform your life."
—**Bill George, Professor, Harvard Business School; former Chair and CEO, Medtronic; and bestselling author of *True North* and *True North Groups***

"This book will help you figure out what really matters in life—and what doesn't matter! This new edition makes a fantastic book even better."
—**Marshall Goldsmith, PhD, bestselling author of *Mojo* and *What Got You Here Won't Get You There***

"If you want to make your life thrive in a deeply purposeful way and live longer and better, you will love this book."
—**Dan Buettner, National Geographic Fellow and *New York Times* bestselling author of *The Blue Zones* and *Thrive***

"Few books are as transformative as this one. The insights gained in *Repacking Your Bags* have changed my own life forever."

—**Tom Kolditz, PhD, Brigadier General (retired); former Head, Department of Behavioral Sciences and Leadership, West Point; and Professor, Practice Management, and Director, Leader Development Program, Yale School of Management**

"*Repacking Your Bags* captures the essence of achieving a good, happily playful, and meaningful life and connects us to our design as humans to 'play' seriously with our destiny. A necessary read!"

—**Stuart L. Brown, MD, founder and President, The National Institute for Play, and author of *Play***

"Richard and David have a wonderful knack for storytelling. This special book is a great companion for the journeys we all continue to take in our lives."

—**Beverly Kaye, founder and CEO, Career Systems International, and bestselling coauthor of *Love 'Em or Lose 'Em***

"*Repacking Your Bags* is a living, breathing, ever-relevant classic. Leider and Shapiro provide the profound yet pragmatic navigation tools to lighten your load, awaken your spirit, and ignite your passionate purpose."

—**Kevin Cashman, bestselling author of *Leadership from the Inside Out***

"Leider and Shapiro have done it again. A powerful tool and support for anyone contemplating life's important questions."

—**Pamela McLean, PhD, CEO, The Hudson Institute of Santa Barbara**

"*Repacking Your Bags* is an indispensable companion during life's many transitions and one of the rare books that I have read and reread many times."

—**Mary Jo Kreitzer, PhD, RN, founder and Director, University of Minnesota's Center for Spirituality and Healing**

"*Repacking Your Bags* is your essential guide to reimagine the next chapter in your life. It is a compass to find the direction of your personal journey."

—**Alex von Bidder, CEO and co-owner, Four Seasons Restaurant, New York City, and Executive Coach**

"Richard Leider and David Shapiro lead us on a personal journey that contains just the right mixture of grace, realism, and hope for a more peaceful and productive future."

—**Larry C. Spears, President, The Spears Center for Servant-Leadership**

"Leider and Shapiro remind us that staying vital, in the present, and hopeful for the future are lifelong activities that demand reflection and determined action. This is a manual for every leader or aspiring agent of change."

—**Clive A. Meanwell, MD, founder, The Medicines Company**

Repacking Your Bags

RICHARD J. LEIDER

DAVID A. SHAPIRO

Repacking Your Bags

LIGHTEN YOUR LOAD

FOR THE GOOD LIFE

THIRD EDITION

BK

Berrett–Koehler Publishers, Inc.
San Francisco
a BK Life book

Berrett-Koehler Publishers, Inc.
235 Montgomery Street, Suite 650
San Francisco, CA 94104-2916
Tel: (415) 288-0260   Fax: (415) 362-2512   www.bkconnection.com

Ordering Information
Quantity sales. Special discounts are available on quantity purchases by corporations, associations, and others. For details, contact the "Special Sales Department" at the Berrett-Koehler address above.

Individual sales. Berrett-Koehler publications are available through most bookstores. They can also be ordered directly from Berrett-Koehler: Tel: (800) 929-2929; Fax: (802) 864-7626; www.bkconnection.com

Orders for college textbook/course adoption use. Please contact Berrett-Koehler: Tel: (800) 929-2929; Fax: (802) 864-7626.

Orders by U.S. trade bookstores and wholesalers. Please contact Ingram Publisher Services, Tel: (800) 509-4887; Fax: (800) 838-1149; E-mail: customer.service@ingrampublisherservices.com; or visit www.ingrampublisherservices.com/Ordering for details about electronic ordering.

Berrett-Koehler and the BK logo are registered trademarks of Berrett-Koehler Publishers, Inc.

Printed in the United States of America

Berrett-Koehler books are printed on long-lasting acid-free paper. When it is available, we choose paper that has been manufactured by environmentally responsible processes. These may include using trees grown in sustainable forests, incorporating recycled paper, minimizing chlorine in bleaching, or recycling the energy produced at the paper mill.

Library of Congress Cataloging-in-Publication Data
Leider, Richard.
Repacking your bags : lighten your load for the good life / by Richard J. Leider & David A. Shapiro. — 3rd ed.
  p. cm.
Includes bibliographical references and index.
ISBN 978-1-60994-549-7 (pbk. : alk. paper)
1. Success—Psychological aspects.   I. Shapiro, David A., 1957–
II. Title.
BF637.S8L435 2012
158—dc23
 2012017869

Third Edition
17 16 15 14 13 12   10 9 8 7 6 5 4 3 2 1

Cover designer: Susan Malikowski, DesignLeaf Studio
Book producer: Detta Penna
Copyeditor: Gail Franklin
Proofreader: Katherine Lee
Indexer: Kirsten Kite

Contents

Why Did We Redo It Again?

The world told us it was time for another edition of this book.

We knew the concept of *Repacking Your Bags* had really arrived when Hollywood got in on the act.

In the 2009 critically-acclaimed film, *Up in the Air,* superstar actor George Clooney plays Ryan Bingham, a corporate downsizing expert who gives motivational speeches on relieving one's life of excess physical and emotional baggage, using the metaphor of unpacking and repacking one's "backpack."

Coincidence? Perhaps.

Plagiarism? Well, we admit it crossed our minds.

But probably the best explanation is that the collective consciousness, or what is sometimes referred to as the "zeitgeist" has, over time, firmly embraced the *Repacking* concept.

In the years since 1994 when *Repacking Your Bags* was first published and 1999 when the second edition came out, we have witnessed the emergence of *Repacking* as a true cultural phenomenon.

Back in the day — the waning years of the 20th century, that is — the ability to "repack," or systematically take stock of one's life and develop an authentic, individualized conception of the good life — was essentially an *option*, mainly for middle-aged people who had achieved a modicum of success in their personal and professional lives. Now, however, well into the second decade of the 21st century, it is an *imperative*, for men and women at all ages and stages. Repacking is an essential survival skill, one required of young job-seekers, midlife career changers, and older adults facing their own challenging transitions to life in a new post-work world.

The tragic events of September 11, 2001 marked a transformation for people not only in the United States, but around the world. Since then, more than ever before, men and women, young and old, are desperate to make sense of their lives. Ironically, more than ever before, people are finding that sense elusive.

Technological advances, major economic shifts, longer life spans, and new attitudes toward aging are revolutionizing the way we live and work. These revolutionary changes are prompting people to ask questions that cut to the core of who we are, individually and as a society.

People feel worn out by overwhelming responsibilities and non-stop changes. We're exhausted — weighed down by shouldering too heavy a load at work, in relationships, and in our communities.

Above all, people have misplaced their sense of fun and play, their native curiosity, their feeling of wonder about the world. Too many of us aren't happy — or at least not as happy as we'd like to be. More and more of us feel a sense of disconnectedness with our work, our relationships, and a deep experience of something larger than ourselves.

The good news is we are all essentially hard-wired to find those connections. We just need a framework, or guidance system, to do so. This new version of *Repacking Your Bags* provides that guidance system, and does so in a way that encourages our natural sense of play and wonder, inspiring us all for the journey ahead.

Countless changes have occurred in the seventeen years since the release of the first edition of *Repacking*. Back in 1994, for instance, hardly anyone we knew had a cell phone, and the internet was still mainly a playground for high-tech geeks. Now, of course, few among us can imagine life without these tools.

The working world has changed radically, too. Lifelong employment at a single company, back then, was still pretty much the norm — or at least the ideal — for most people. Now it's as quaint a business notion as the secretarial typing pool. Globalization has gone from being a visionary buzzword to a fact of life for companies everywhere. In fact, it is so ingrained that it is a target of protest by people seriously questioning the meaning and purpose of today's corporations. Financial crisis has become the "new normal." Millions of people have been downsized, upsized, rightsized, and resized as gyrations in the marketplace continue to buffet companies and organizations of every size.

In our own lives, the changes, though smaller, have been scarcely less dramatic. Both of us, upon completing the first edition of *Repacking,* made a conscious choice to dramatically reconfigure our personal and professional lives in an effort to more fully realize our vision of the good life: *Living in the place you belong, with the people you love, doing the right work, on purpose.*

And following the release of the second edition of *Repacking,* we have continued to evaluate and re-evaluate our lives with those four areas in mind. We've both been persistently repacking as needed, to pursue the good life as each of us sees it.

Richard restructured his corporate coaching practice to focus more on writing and speaking. Dave finished his stint as a graduate student in philosophy, and is now a tenured college instructor in his chosen field. Richard, who had initially responded to his renewed sense of place by relocating to a rural home on the banks of the St. Croix River, also found he sometimes belonged at a small *pied à terre* condo nearer to his office in the Twin Cities of Minneapolis/St. Paul. Dave bought a house, something for years he had vowed he would never do.

Even our purposes continue to be revised and revitalized. Richard, who had originally defined his purpose as "to help people discover and express their essence," and later, more simply as "uncovering callings," has now repacked his purpose as "awakening spirit." In other words, he now envisions his life's purpose as empowering others to develop a vision of their life's purpose. Dave, who had seen himself primarily as a writer, and then mainly as a professional academic philosopher, now conceives his purpose in terms of teaching and facilitating educational experiences with young people. He defines it, in terms of a calling, as "fostering dialogue."

Throughout our changes we have found ourselves again and again still unpacking; still reflecting on who we are and why. Still looking over what we're carrying, and asking ourselves if we still need it for the journey ahead.

At each crossroad, we have examined our lives and our options in light of the lessons of *Repacking.* We have wondered what we needed to make ourselves happy: what to bring along and what to leave behind, what to acquire and what to give away, what to do and with whom to do it.

Individually we experienced the joys and challenges of repacking: the struggles to figure out what really matters, and the sense of liberation that comes from making choices that express who we really are in our personal and professional lives. We also heard from literally thousands of readers who had repacked their own bags and now wanted to share stories of their challenges and triumphs along the way.

As we noted in the second edition of *Repacking,* one of the most compelling lessons that emerged for us is that the process is not something that happens once and is done with. It's an experience that stays with you, that stimulates thinking and inspires ongoing reflection.

What has come home to us even more clearly is how much we

underestimated the value and imperative of continually repacking. It is not, as we once imagined, a matter of mid-course corrections. Rather, repacking is a navigational imperative. None of us can get where we hope to without frequently reconsidering where we're going and how to get there.

We've come to understand that repacking is a *lifelong* process. We need to be continually engaged in it so as to stay vital, fully alive in the present, and hopeful for the future.

We had originally thought of repacking as something people do once (or at most, a couple of times) in *reaction* to a sense of disillusionment or frustration in their lives. Now we understand it much more clearly as a *proactive* process. We've found that with each step along the way it remains necessary to re-examine what has brought us here, to continue asking ourselves if the choices that have sustained us so far are continuing to do so — or if they're just weighing us down.

And while this does entail a deep questioning, it's a kind of questioning we've found that we can't really live without — not if we want to *feel* alive.

As we approach this revision of *Repacking,* we are no longer young; indeed, we have both entered the "country of old men." Dave is well into his fifties and Richard qualified for Medicare almost five years ago. We are both card-carrying members of AARP. And yet both of us still feel young — especially in two ways.

First, we share a sense of vitality that seems to come from a willingness to reimagine our lives. And second, we feel young in the sense of not really knowing, or claiming to know. We realize, as a result of our own repackings, that life still is, and will always be, a process of discovery. It has become more obvious to us than ever that repacking is not essentially about reaching the destination, but about the learning journey.

We are reminded that the keys to this discovery process lie within us. To feel fully alive we must repeatedly turn our gaze inward. To know where we are on the trip, where we want to go, and how to get there, we must learn to count on an inner sense of direction.

Quite simply, we must continually unpack and repack our bags.

"Unpacking" simply means taking a long, hard look at what we're carrying and why. Seeing if our possessions, relationships, purpose and work are still helping us move forward, or if they're weighing us down.

"Repacking," then, is the ongoing and continuous activity of reflection and choice. Rearranging our priorities. Reframing our vision of the good life. And recovering a new sense of being alive.

This book was originally written as a chronicle of our own repacking. This revision revisits that chronicle and expands upon it by referencing unpacking and repacking episodes that have emerged in the years since. In the nearly two decades since *Repacking* first came out, we've often been enlightened — but more often, humbled — by others' experiences with it. As a result, and due, in part, to our ongoing efforts to repack our own bags, we both think we've developed a further understanding of the good life and how to go about attaining it.

We offer this revised chronicle as the current version of a guidebook to the future for our fellow travelers. May it help you lighten your step on the road to the good life.

The Question That Started It All ...

Does all this make you happy?
— Maasai elder

Richard explains how it all began.

Late one afternoon, on a trek through the highlands along the edge of the Serengeti Plains in East Africa, I experience a breakthrough.

East Africa is suffering one of the worst droughts in history. The vast plains are parched, stripped to dust. River beds run bone dry. Fields of lush grass have been reduced to patches of stiff straw, and the myriad flowers, normally painted in deep shades of green, blue, and mauve, are bleached of all color. Only the dust devils, whirling high overhead and then touching down on the hard, fractured ground, seem to prosper.

In the distance, over the scorched Serengeti, move enormous herds of animals— more than a million and a half strong— coming together in search of water and food, tracing the hoof-worn trails that are the highways of their migratory route. They pour steadily across the plains in a broad stream several miles long. It is an extraordinary spectacle, unlike anything else on earth.

The sun is setting, creating water mirages that appear and disappear before our eyes. But the intense heat lingers like a bad dream. It has drained us of all energy. We ride along in our Land Rover, like so many rag dolls strapped in our seats. Small cracks in the vehicle's frame vacuum in clouds of dust that blanket us. The fine silt seeps into our pores until our own bodies feel as dry as the surrounding terrain.

As the leader of this group of twelve midlife adventurers who have traveled 7000 miles on this "Inventure Expedition" to come face-to-face with Africa and themselves, I feel especially exhausted. The responsibility of assuring their safety and continued involvement in our process is, at times, almost as oppressive as the heat.

We pull into Magaduru, a small Maasai village in the highlands above the Serengeti. We will be camping here for the night before the start of our backpacking trek in the morning.

A tall, lean Maasai man of aristocratic bearing springs upon our group. He plunges the shaft of his spear into the ground and stands in the pose of the heron, balancing on one foot, bracing the other on the inner thigh of the supporting leg. He adjusts the small sword that hangs on his waist, then throws a worn blanket around his body, with a confidence that imparts style and grace to this simple gesture. His dark, penetrating eyes survey us as if scouting the windswept plain that lies behind. No emotion is revealed on his proud, serious face.

Then suddenly, he breaks into a broad smile and greets us in English and Kiswahili.

"*Jambo!* Welcome to my *boma!*"

He talks rapidly with our guide, David Peterson, first fixing his gaze on us, then nodding in the direction of his nearby cattle. Loud laughter erupts from the bushes where women and children are hiding.

"What is he saying?" we ask.

David smiles. "He hopes the smell of cattle dung is not too strong for you!"

This breaks the ice. Our laughter fills the air, joining that of our greeter. He introduces himself as Thaddeus Ole Koyie, the village leader. Gripping my hands firmly, he invites our group to be his guests.

In the lively conversation that follows, Koyie, who will be our Maasai guide for the upcoming trek, tells us that he has been educated at missionary school, where he learned to speak English. He does not explain, though, why he has turned his back on "modern" ways. Clearly, he is an influential elder, particularly for a man who is only forty. But there is something more and it implies a powerful sense of place and deep contentment with village life.

The Maasai are intensely communicative in the company of people they know. For reasons of their own, however, they are aloof and suspicious toward strangers. Happily, we don't remain strangers for long.

All of us are quite taken with Koyie. A gregarious and witty man, he has the uncanny ability to move easily between the two worlds of our group and his village, transcending the barriers of language and custom. That night, around the small campfire, when he speaks of the drought, tears glisten in his eyes. Through his passionate eloquence we come to understand that drought, to the Maasai, is very nearly a death sentence.

Early next morning, as we leave Koyie's *boma* on our trek, I proudly sport a brand-new backpack. It is one of those high-tech ultra-light models designed for maximum cargo-carrying efficiency. You know the kind — covered with snaps, clasps, and zippers, full of pockets and pouches, compartments inside compartments, a veritable Velcro heaven — and I have the thing stuffed. I'm a walking advertisement for a Patagonia or L.L. Bean catalogue. But of course, I have to be. As expedition leader, I'm responsible for the entire group. So, in addition to the required group-size first aid kit, I've also been sure to bring along items that will make our trek not just safe, but enjoyable. I'm no Boy Scout, but I certainly subscribe to the motto, "Be prepared." And I have made it a point to be prepared for just about anything.

As we walk along, Koyie keeps glancing at my pack. Time and again, I see him mentally comparing the heavy load I carry with his own, which is nothing more than a spear and a stick used for cattle-tending. Eventually we get to talking about my backpack, and he expresses his eagerness to see its contents. Pleased at how impressed he appears to be, I offer to show him my stuff. I look forward to letting him see how carefully I've prepared for our journey and how ready for anything I am.

The opportunity presents itself late that afternoon as we are setting up camp near another *boma.* Proudly I commence to lay out for him everything in my pack. I unsnap snaps, unzip zippers, and un-Velcro Velcro. From pouches, pockets, and compartments I produce all sorts of strange and wonderful items. Eating utensils, cutting devices, digging tools. Direction finders, star gazers, map readers. Things to write with, on, and for. Various garments in various sizes for various functions. Medical supplies, remedies, and cures. Little bottles inside little bottles inside little bottles. Waterproof bags for everything. Amazing stuff!

At length I have all the gear spread out. It looks like that photo they always have in the centerfold of "great explorer" articles, that shows everything necessary for a successful trip to the farthest reaches of the planet. Needless to say I'm pretty satisfied with my collection.

I look over at Koyie to gauge his reaction. He seems amused, but he is silent. I understand. Surveying the items arrayed about us, I don't know quite what to say, either.

Finally, after several minutes of just gazing at everything, Koyie turns to me and asks very simply, but with great intensity:

"Does all this make you happy?"

There was something very powerful about Koyie's question. His words seemed to hit right at the heart of my deepest values. I honestly couldn't answer him that evening, and even weeks afterwards, I couldn't completely say for sure.

In a split second his question had gotten me to think about all that I was carrying and why — not just on our trek, but through my entire life.

Compelled by a need to explain it to Koyie — and myself — I immediately began going through all that I had, trying to decide if it *did* make me happy. He and I sat around the fire and talked long into the night. As he listened to me, I listened also, for I found that I was clarifying the essentials of my life.

In response to the question I began to realize the truth. Some of the things did make me happy, but many of them didn't — at least not in any way that made sense to be dragging them along. So as I repacked I set those things aside, and eventually, gave them to the local villages. I went on the rest of the trek without them. I'm not sure that I'll never want or need them again, but I certainly didn't suffer for not having them at the time.

My load was much lighter after I'd re-examined my needs. And on the rest of the trip, I was quite a bit happier for having repacked my bags.

As a result of this experience I began to assemble my thoughts and feelings about how to lighten my life's load. The insight I've gained has contributed to, and been informed by, my work as a life coach. In discussions with clients, colleagues, and family members I've developed a new understanding of how important it is to regularly *unpack* and *repack* our bags throughout our lives.

As my co-author, David, and I have worked with these thoughts, we've made a number of discoveries that are at the core of this book.

- We've discovered that many people are laboring through their lives, weighed down by attachments that no longer serve them. Patterns of behavior that have helped them get where they are, aren't helping them get where they want to be. As a result, many people feel overwhelmed. At the same time, many are questioning the point of it all. They're wondering if what they're working so hard for is really worth it. Time and again we hear people say things something like, "I don't even feel like I'm living my life. What's it all for? What is my true purpose? What is my life really all about?" In short, we hear them asking for a sense of authenticity: a clearly rendered, easily understandable, and most importantly, *individualized* conception of happiness or the good life. This is what we explore in Chapter 1, *What Is the Good Life?*

- We've discovered that it is possible to simplify one's life without sacrificing the conveniences and comforts we've come to expect. We can *give up* without *giving in.* By having less *in* our lives, we can get more *out of* life. To get to this place, we have to figure out what really matters. We have to examine what's in our bags and decide for ourselves if it's really what we want to be carrying. This is the focus of Chapter 2, *Unpacking Your Bags.*

- We've developed a new appreciation for what the "good life" entails and how important it is that, in creating a vision of the good life for ourselves, we take into account four critical factors: Work, Love, Place, and Purpose. The first three of these are considered in turn, in Chapter 3, *Repacking Your Place Bag,* Chapter 4, *Repacking Your Relationship Bag, and* Chapter 5, *Repacking Your Work Bag.*

- We've learned that it's not just *what* we carry "in our bags" that determines the quality of our lives; it's also, more importantly, *why* we carry what we do. That's the Purpose component. It's vital to become clear about our life's purpose so that we can carry what we're carrying with balance, fortitude, and joy. With that in mind, we've found that happiness has more to do with experiencing than with having. Having is great, but it's not *it.* For most of us, what we're really looking for is a feeling — a feeling of aliveness. This is what Chapter 6, *Repacking On Purpose,* is all about.

- Finally, we've come to understand that repacking is a process that doesn't end; it's a mindset and an approach to living that goes on continually. Living with passion and purpose means that we must consistently re-evaluate our lives and make changes — usually subtle, but sometimes more significant — to rebalance what we're carrying and why. This is the focus of Chapter 7, *The Freedom of the Road*, as well as the Epilogue, *Lightening Your Load.*

Over the past two decades we've thought a lot about the lessons of *Repacking,* and our questions and our learning have continued. The conversations we've had sitting around late night fires and trekking across windswept plains have given us insight into ourselves and our culture. These experiences remind us that the freedom to choose is not something we *have* — and can therefore lose — but something we *are*. It is of our deepest essence, just waiting to be unpacked.

At every moment, in every situation, we are free to choose a simpler expression of our being. We always have the potential to unpack, lighten our loads, and repack.

For many of us it takes a crisis, midlife or other, to get us even thinking about what we're carrying. And then, unfortunately, we tend to make decisions from within the crisis. Instead of pausing to reconsider, in a purposeful manner, what we've brought along and why, we're apt to cast everything off and just run. Instead of making rational decisions that prepare us for what's ahead, we tend to come from a position of panic or fear — and the choices we make reflect that.

We can use a process for repacking our bags to stimulate thought on this issue in calmer times. We can reflect on our lives in a manner that helps us sort out what's really important — what makes us happy — from what's just weighing us down. We can then map out a new road ahead, one that will get us where we really want to go, with the things we really want to bring along the way.

And that, in a nutshell — or should we say backpack — is what this book is all about.

So Who Needs This Book?

Increasingly of late, people have shared with us questions like these:

- "What's next for me?"
- "Why doesn't all this make me happy?"
- "Who do I want to be when I grow up?"
- "How can I find my life's work?"
- "How can I re-imagine my life?"

If any of these echo your own feelings, then *Repacking Your Bags: Lighten Your Load for the Good Life* is for you.

It's particularly appropriate if you find yourself at a place in your life where past patterns are weighing you down. If the person you've always been isn't the person you want to be at this point in your life.

This isn't a book for people who believe that lightening their load means they have to sell all their possessions and move to the woods or an ashram in India. It's for people involved in the day-to-day struggle of juggling work, home, and relationship demands in a way that enables them to make ends meet while burning the candle at both.

Repacking is for businesspeople, professionals, homemakers, students, and retirees — in short, everyone who needs to prepare for and embrace what's next in their lives.

For those of you facing midlife and beyond — no doubt a very different sort of second half than previous generations faced — *Repacking* may have special appeal. Similarly, for those of you just starting out in your adult lives, *Repacking* can offer guidance and direction you may find particularly useful. Finally, if you're someone who has recently experienced (or is about to experience) a major transition in your life — a job loss, a relocation, a relationship change — then *Repacking* can act as a compass as you get your bearings for the journey ahead.

Repacking starts with the assumption that everyone has a different definition of the good life. Therefore, in order to achieve an authentic experience of our own good life, each of us must reflect and choose. *Repacking* offers an approach to do that — an approach that is innovative in three ways.

First, by providing a generic formula for the good life into which you can plug your own specifics, *Repacking* enables you to shape your own vision of what the good life means to you, personally.

Second, *Repacking* encourages you to reflect on and commit to your vision of the good life through an emphasis on "courageous conversation" — with yourself and others.

Third, *Repacking* uses the metaphor of travel to help remind you that life is a journey and that your experience on the way is inextricably bound up in the baggage — emotional, intellectual, and physical — that you are carrying.

Essentially, it's about choice — but choice that springs from inner needs and a whole person perspective.

The ability to repack our bags and make choices that move us in new, more fulfilling directions is a power that lies within us all. Our experience with Repacking Your Bags has helped us do that, and we hope that your experience with Repacking can do the same for you.

Ultimately, we're all in transition — always. And what repacking as a metaphor teaches us is that having a process to help navigate those transitions is the key to living our ongoing vision of the good life.

Of course, there are many ways to engage that process and you'll discover your own as you proceed. But perhaps the best way to get going is to begin with the question at the root of it all:

Does all this make you happy?

CHAPTER 1

What Is the Good Life?

In the Woody Allen movie, *Midnight in Paris,* Owen Wilson plays Gil, a successful Hollywood screenwriter visiting Paris with his fiancé, Inez. Gil, who is struggling to complete his first novel, falls in love with the city, and fantasizes about moving there, a prospect Inez, who can hardly wait to get back to Southern California, considers just silly romantic nonsense.

Although Inez's dismissal of Gil's dream is a symptom of deeper problems in their relationship, she has a point. Because it's not even contemporary Paris that Gil adores — not the Paris of the 21st century — rather, he has fallen in love with a dream: Paris of the 1920s, the Paris of Ernest Hemingway, F. Scott and Zelda Fitzgerald, Gertrude Stein, and the whole Lost Generation of Americans who made the City of Lights their home after World War I.

In fact, so powerfully does Gil long for this time that one night, to his surprise and consternation, he is magically transported back to that world: he is picked up at midnight by Scott and Zelda and taken in a limousine to a party, where he meets such luminaries as Cole Porter, Josephine Baker, and of course, Hemingway himself. At first, understandably, he can't believe what is happening, but eventually, he comes to accept that it's real, and is thrilled by his good fortune.

The next night, he invites Inez to accompany him, but she tires and goes home before the magical limousine appears. When it does, at midnight, Gil goes off alone into the past, and Hemingway takes him to the salon of Gertrude Stein, who to Gil's delight, agrees to read and critique his novel. He meets Salvador Dali and Pablo Picasso, and most significantly, makes the acquaintance of a beautiful young woman, Adriana, Picasso's muse and lover. We come to know that her relationship with the famous artist is tumultuous and certain to end badly, soon. But for Gil, it is love at first sight; he can't get her out of his mind, even when he returns, in the morning, to his contemporary life.

Gil makes up excuses to Inez so he can keep going back to the past. And what transpires is that he comes to see his life there, back in the 1920s, as his "real" life. So desperately has he wanted to live a life that wasn't his own, a life that he has glamorized as more beautiful, more poetic, more meaningful than the one he has made for himself, that, soon, he has fully embraced that world, so much so that he wants to stay there always.

He begins an affair with Adriana, who, as predicted, has been dumped by Picasso. They share their hopes and dreams, Gil revealing his belief that Paris of the 1920s is the perfect world, the time and place where art, culture, and society reached their apex. Adriana, by contrast, contends that it was Paris of La Belle Epoque, the time of Impressionism and Art Nouveau, when the city was at its apogee.

And indeed, so fervent is her desire for that lost time, that one night, as she and Gil stroll along, a horse-drawn carriage appears and transports them back to a café in Montmartre, circa 1870, where they meet the famous painters Claude Monet and Henri de Toulouse-Lautrec. Unfortunately for Gil, Adriana decides to remain back in her idealized Paris; she bids Gil adieu and he returns to the present, once and for all.

Although he is saddened by the break-up, he arrives at a new and profound understanding of himself and his life. He realizes that in his desire to escape the present and flee to an image of a world he believed to be better than his own, he was reaching for something ephemeral and ultimately, unreal. He was imagining himself to be someone he wasn't, trying desperately to fit into a place that, in the end, he didn't belong. In short, he was being inauthentic, or to put it another way, he was striving for a version of the good life that wasn't really his own.

Back in the present, he decides to stay in Paris after all, break off his engagement with Inez (with whom he realizes he has little in common), and pursue his true passion of novel-writing, even if it turns out to be less profitable than being a Hollywood hack.

As the film ends, we see Gil striking up an acquaintance with an attractive woman he has met briefly in an antiquities shop during his time in contemporary Paris. We don't know how their relationship will unfold — and neither does Gil — but we get a sense that whatever happens to our hero, it will spring from the true core of his character, and an authentic expression of who he really is.

Over the years, we've met many people who are in the same place as Gil was during his sojourn into the past. They seem like they're not really living their real lives. They're reaching for a vision of a lost world, one they're trying to grasp by adopting a lifestyle that isn't their own. It's as if by embracing someone else's conception of how life should be led, they'll discover for themselves the life they want. But as a result, they never quite feel fully at home with themselves. They feel dull — and dulled. They feel trapped, insulated. They "go through the motions" of living, but there's no life in their lives.

We hear their dissatisfaction expressed in a several different ways:

- "I'm so busy these days. I don't know how to have fun any more."

- Or, "I wish my life was different, like a character in a movie or on TV."

- Or, "It's just the same thing day after day. I never do anything that's fun."

That's not quite true. Many of these people have lots of fun. They've got their garages filled with all kinds of fun stuff: golf clubs, jet skis, mountain bikes, you name it. In fact, for many of them, "fun" has become an addiction. But as with most addictive substances, people build up a tolerance to it. So despite all the "fun" people have, they're still not happy.

What's really missing is a sense of joy. People find that they no longer feel authentic joy in living, despite all the fun stuff they have or do. And this is the case whether they're male or female, young or old, rich or poor, or at any stage of life.

What's happened to people is that they've lost a delicate, but critical, component of aliveness and well-being: they've lost their uniqueness, their *authenticity*. It happens to many of us as we grow up and make our way in the world. We fit in. We see how other people survive and adopt their strategies to preserve our jobs, our incomes, and our relationships. Swept along by the myriad demands of day-to-day living, we stop making choices of our own. Or even realizing that we have choices to make.

We lose the wonderful weird edges that define us. We cover up the eccentricities that make us unique. Alfred Adler, the great 20th century psychologist and educator, considered these eccentricities a vital part of a happy and fulfilling lifestyle. Ironically, the very term he coined — "lifestyle" — has come to imply something almost entirely opposite to eccentricity. These days it suggests a pre-configured package formatted for easy consumption. "Lifestyle" now refers to things that we buy; someone else's idea of what we need to be happy. But is anyone really satisfied with these mass-marketed ideas of happiness? Is anyone really nourished by a life that isn't authentic?

Why Do We Feel So Bad?

Everywhere we look, we see people pursuing happiness, as if it's something they could capture and cage. But pinning happiness down only destroys it. It's too wild for that — it needs room to roam. You have to give it time, let it wander, let it surprise you. You have to discover what it means to you *authentically*, rather than trying to adopt a version of it from someone else.

Dave was reminded of this when, upon Richard's recommendation, he went to see *Midnight In Paris*.

That was me, as a young man. I lived that experience, just like Gil. Right after my wife, Jennifer, and I were married, we sold everything we owned and moved to Paris, in hopes of finding something. But the search was doomed, because what I was looking for was something that didn't come from within. Rather, it was an image of a life — or of a lifestyle, really — that I thought would make me happy. But I didn't realize that as long as it was someone else's image, that would never be so.

The lifestyle I lusted after was that of the Henry-Miller-meets-Jim-Morrison expatriate poet/writer, eking out a living on the fringes of society. I wanted an alternative lifestyle, but I didn't want to have to invent my own alternatives.

When we got to Paris, I bought into the whole "tortured artist" scene. I dressed only in black, and even took up smoking cigarettes to complete the picture. I refused to do anything that might contrast with this image, even things that might possibly have been fun. So, for instance, in no way would I consider visiting the Eiffel Tower. That was only for tourists, for the bourgeoisie, for simple-minded Americans (I pretended I wasn't one) looking for enjoyment. I did my best to sustain this attitude in spite of the dreary time I was having in one of the greatest cities in the world. In fact, I might have been fairly miserable the entire time that Jen and I lived over there, were it not for one moment when my dark veneer of self-importance sustained a major — and truly enlightening — crack.

I was sitting in a café, nursing a glass of Bordeaux, affecting a pose of resigned world-weariness. I observed the passersby outside on the street going through the pointless motions of human life, and my heart was filled with deep existential despair. A small dog appeared, and while I watched, deposited a large turd on the sidewalk just in front of the cafe entrance. It seemed to me to be the perfect metaphor for the filth and degradation of everyday existence.

I ordered another glass of wine and resolved to sit and watch until someone stepped into the mess, feeling that this would sum up perfectly how we move through our days — blithely wandering along until, all of a sudden, and for no reason at all, we are soiled with foul and noxious excrement.

The show turned out to be quite amusing — and exciting as hell. Person after person would almost step into it, but at the last second, either notice and move aside or luckily, just miss it. It was like watching a daredevil high wire act at the circus. I started to have a great time. I was smiling, laughing out loud. I even stopped smoking.

The patron of the cafe, who had always seemed to me to be this forbidding character, came over to me, lured by my good humor. We got into a great conversation about philosophy and American baseball. He introduced me to his wife, who, after remarking that I was too thin, went away and returned with a bowl of the most delicious potato stew I have ever tasted. The patron broke out a special bottle of wine that we shared with great conviviality. I talked to more people that evening than I had in the entire five previous months, and somewhere along the line, forgot all about my artistic angst.

I ended up closing down the cafe, and after bidding a fond adieu to my new friends, stepped merrily out the door . . . and right into the pile of dog-doo. The joke was on me — literally.

That was the loudest I laughed all night. In that moment I came to the full realization that I didn't have to be someone I thought I should be; instead, I could allow myself to be the person I really was. The goal wasn't to adopt an image drawn from my impression of someone else; rather, it was to let my own authentic self emerge from real-life experiences. For the first time since I had arrived in Paris, I finally felt like myself. And from that day on, for the rest of our time there, I resolved to live my own life, not someone else's.

A Simple Formula for What's Not So Simple

To put it simply, the formula for the good life is:

Living in the place you belong,
with the people you love,
doing the right work,
on purpose.

What does this mean? Above all, it means, as mentioned above, an integration. A sense of harmony among the various components in one's life. It means that, for example, the place where you live provides adequate opportunities for you to do the kind of work you want to do. That your work gives you time to be with the people you really love. And that your deepest friendships contribute to the sense of community you feel in the place where you live and work.

The thread that holds the good life together is purpose. Defining your sense of purpose — your thread — enables you to continually travel in the direction of your vision of the good life. It helps you keep focusing on where you want to go and discovering new roads to get there.

In seminars and workshops Richard often uses a poem by the poet William Stafford to illustrate this idea. The poem, called "The Way It Is," introduces the notion of a thread that we follow, that goes among things that change in our lives but that doesn't itself change. We will meet challenges, joys, and tragedies along the way, but the thread runs through it all — and we never let go of that thread.

We understand the good life, therefore, as a journey, held together by a common thread. It's not something we achieve once and hold onto forever. It keeps changing throughout our lives. The balance among place, love, and work is always shifting. At some stages, we'll be especially focused on work issues. At others we'll be more concerned with developing a sense of place, putting down roots, creating a home for ourselves. And most of us know what it's like to have love as our number one concern — maybe all too well.

When we're clear about our purpose, though, it's easier to establish and maintain the necessary sense of balance. Purpose is what keeps us from getting too far sidetracked by issues related to place, love, or work. It provides perspective and a thread to galvanize our choices. And something to reach for as we start letting go.

Letting Go

It's a difficult truth — the good life requires personal courage. No one else can define it for you. The blessing of this is that there's never anyone stopping you from making the effort. The curse is that there's no one stopping you but yourself.

It takes some serious unpacking — letting go — to move forward on the trip.

To unpack is to awaken; to see something different; to ask new questions. It is an expression of an urge to create, to live whole.

Time and time again, the world's greatest artists, musicians, sculptors, inventors, scientists, explorers, writers and so forth have testified to the "unpacking" dimension of this creative process. "Regular folks" have, too.

The late Linda Jadwin, a former corporate executive with a major technology firm in the Midwest, said:

> When I was a young girl I learned how to swim in a swamp. I was drawn to the mysterious odors and strange textures of its murky depths. I can still remember how it felt to paddle through the cool water while slippery, slimy fish eggs slid around my back and tall grass gashed my arms and legs. There was life and death there in that swamp — birth and decay. The red-winged blackbirds perched on the cattails watched me with apparent disdain. Dragonflies dived and buzzed at my head. Tadpoles and minnows tickled me as they swam about. The mud and goo that oozed between my toes was like heaven itself. I loved it there, immersed in the juice and slime of it, stinking to high heaven. That was the good life to me.

At 50, Linda still felt the need to swim in that swamp.

> I've proven I can function well in the world. Now it's time to return to the swamp. I want more experiences like that, that make my hair stand on end.
>
> From 50, I can see time better — past and future — and can get in touch with the small speck I am and feel both the importance and unimportance of my life.
>
> I don't know who I want to "be" next. I feel like I'm on a path. I made a big shift last year. I thought through what I'd do if I got downsized or fired. I asked every possible question of myself and others. It freed me up and gave me a sense of peace. I feel I can accept anything that comes along now — meet it and even greet it.
>
> When I turned 50, I had no idea I'd get so much pleasure out of my own imagination — my own private world. That's been the greatest joy of my life. I always thought the good life

was attached to achievements or adventure. But now I realize that the good life is being in the swamp, feeling everything deeply.

Great breakthroughs result from a single moment in which a person lets go of their usual assumptions and looks at things from a new point of view.

Creating the good life is a similar process. Life can never be adequately discussed or conceptualized, but only created — by living in our own questions, by continually unpacking and repacking our bags.

D. T. Suzuki, an author of books and essays on Zen Buddhism, said, "I'm an artist at living, and my work of art is my life."

People who are "artists at living" are bold enough to question the status quo — to accept that someone else's truth could be a lie for them. They are also willing to recognize when their own truths have become a dead end, in which case they demonstrate the courage to let go. They accept what they can from an experience and move on.

People do not always make breakthroughs because they *refused* to quit. Sometimes they make them because they know *when* to quit. When they realize that enough is enough, that old patterns aren't serving them, that it's time to repack their bags.

The Biggest of the Big Questions

We have defined the good life as "Living in the place I belong, with the people I love, doing the right work, on purpose." As we see it, place, relationships, work, and purpose are the cornerstones of a well-lived life. Although we have tried to present this as clearly and creatively as possible, there's really nothing all that groundbreaking about our definition. Philosophers, artists, theologians, and other thoughtful people have wondered and written about the good life for centuries — and, for the most part, their answers are not all that different from our own.

Among the best-known historical discussions of the good life is found in Aristotle's *Nichomachean Ethics.* In this classic work, written around 330 B.C., Aristotle wonders about the biggest of the "big" philosophical questions: "What is the meaning of life?" He reasons that, since everything everyone does is ultimately aimed at happiness, that the meaning of life — the reason we are all here — is happiness. Of course, if this is the case, we still have to define what happiness really is.

Aristotle rejects the usual definitions of happiness: pleasure, honor, and wealth. The life of pleasure isn't authentically happy for a couple of reasons. First, if all we strive for is sensual pleasure then we're really no better than beasts. Humans clearly have greater potential for meaningful lives; a life of pure pleasure is unworthy of what's best about us. Second, as we all know, the single-minded pursuit of pleasure is self-defeating. Overindulgence in the sensual pleasures always leads to hangovers of one sort or another; we end up feeling worse — and less happy — than we did before we started seeking pleasure.

The pursuit of honor doesn't yield authentic happiness for Aristotle, primarily because honor is so dependent upon what other people think of us. If we think that being famous will make us happy, we're constantly going to be at the mercy of other people's opinions. And this is undoubtedly a recipe for unhappiness, if not downright disaster.

Finally, wealth can't be the definition of happiness for an obvious reason: no one (or at least no reasonable person) seeks wealth for its own sake. The only reason we want to be rich is so that we can be free to do certain things. Therefore, argues Aristotle, money can't be synonymous with happiness because, unlike happiness, it's not something we aspire to as an end in itself.

From this, Aristotle comes to a different conception of happiness, which is best defined using the original Greek term, *eudaimonia.* *Eudaimonia,* for Aristotle, isn't something we attain; rather, happiness, or the good life, is an *activity*. As Aristotle conceives of it, *eudaimonia* is activity of the soul in accordance with human beings' special virtue, rational activity. Ultimately, then, happiness is going to be the ongoing activity of exercising moral and intellectual virtue. In other words, happiness is going to be doing what we are meant to do, in the best way possible.

So, after all, this isn't very different from the way we've defined the good life in this book. Like Aristotle, we agree that the good life isn't something you *get;* it's something you *do*. It involves living, relating, and working *on purpose*. It isn't about what we have or what people think of us; it's about how we live our lives.

We also agree with Aristotle (and many other well-known thinkers throughout history) that real happiness comes from setting our own lives within a larger context. While it's certainly the case that our happiness flows from the fulfillment of our individual interests and desires, it's equally obvious that there's something more; something bigger than our particular perspective on things. There are, of course, innumerably different modes of living, all of them viable in themselves. But at the same time, it's clear that *every* life, however it is lived, needs to have certain elements for an individual's satisfaction and happiness. A life lived without connection to this larger context is missing something deeper, and ultimately, something essential to real happiness.

The connection between an individual's vision of one's own good life and the good life in general is difficult to make, but we strongly believe that it needs to be done.

Testing Our Edges

Unfortunately, very few of us have anything in our development that provides us with the knowledge and skills to unpack and repack our bags. The self-awareness required to know *what* to pack and the discipline needed to realize what to *leave behind* typically come totally as a result of trial and error, or what can be called "testing our edges."

People like Linda Jadwin, with the courage to "test their edges," eventually break through to greater aliveness and fulfillment. People who "stay packed" out of fear or unwillingness to let go gain only a false sense of security. By covering up, wearing masks, and shutting down, they eventually experience a kind of death: the death of self-respect.

To succeed in the 21st century we must learn to unpack and re-pack our bags — often. To do this, we must ask the right questions.

These questions are trail markers on our journey. They may not always point us in the right direction, but if we ask them and seek their answers with energy and creativity, they will help keep us moving forward.

With that in mind, you are encouraged to turn now to the *Repacking Journal* and complete *The Good Life Inventory*. It only takes a few moments, and will help clarify what the good life is for you.

Postcards and Repacking Partners

Below is the first of several *Postcard Exercises* you will find in this book.

These exercises are designed to remind you that life is a journey, and that it's important to include others in it, to let them know where you are and how things are going on the way.

Postcards are an especially quick and easy way to correspond with friends, family, and colleagues. Writing a postcard is a lot more personal than just firing off an email. And usually it's much more effective in communicating something you really feel. Reaching out to make contact is what matters. It's not necessarily WHAT you say, but simply THAT you say it.

It's about getting the conversation going.

Conversation lies at the very foundation of all Western culture. Our religious and philosophical traditions are rooted in dialogue. Ironically, though, one of the most common complaints we hear about contemporary society is that no one talks any more.

Friends, clients, business associates all echo the same refrain. No one has time for a real heart-to-heart. We have dozens and dozens of "friends" on Facebook, but hardly any real friends to whom we can authentically reveal ourselves. And when we do get together to talk, it's about things: work, sports, fashion, TV. Anything to keep the conversation light and lively and away from what's really going on. Meanwhile, what we really want to talk about is life — our lives — in depth.

Nietzsche wrote about marriage as "a long conversation." Many marriages quickly descend into short-tempered comments or, just as often, total silence.

The same goes for many work relationships. The two most courageous conversations most people have with anyone at their work are their initial interview and their exit interview. In between, they're too busy hurrying through the day.

Meanwhile, people really want to talk. They need to. It's a human instinct as powerful as hunger or thirst; we all need to tell our story and have it be heard.

That's why this book puts such an emphasis on conversation. The exercises and activities around unpacking and repacking are intended to be done with a partner, or partners, and to stimulate discussion about the issues in question. Consider them a map for your conversations, but don't hesitate to stray off the beaten path if that's where they take you.

This isn't to say that you can't do the exercises on your own. Going through the process of completing them will definitely make a difference. But if you can get a dialogue going with someone else, someone who can reflect back to you what you've expressed, you'll learn more about yourself than you would otherwise. And probably have more fun doing it, as well.

So we really encourage you to SEND the postcards you write. Use them to get a conversation going with your postcard penpal.

Choose your postcard penpal — a person we call your Repacking Partner — based on the subject of the postcard you're sending. This means you might have a number of different Repacking Partners. That's okay. But it's also okay if you only have one.

The main thing about postcards is that they are concise. Each postcard is meant to be a quick note, a "snapshot" of where you are. Don't agonize over a long, involved letter that you'll never get around to finishing. Focus instead on a simple, straightforward message that opens the door to further conversation.

The postcards can be a catalyst for longer talks — like the ones you have when you've sent a postcard to someone, and then visit them after your trip and see the postcard on their refrigerator. It reminds you of the experience, and gives you a chance to fill in the details, and get a real conversation going about what happened and how you felt about it. Postcards sure beat the standard email exchanges we usually have.

What Is the Good Life?
Postcard Directions

First, think about the following:

- Are you living your own vision of the good life, or somebody else's?

  o my own   o someone else's   o a combination

- Are you facing the Two Deadly Fears? *(see chapter 6)*

  o Fear 1   o Fear 2   o neither

- Are you having more or less fun than you did a year ago?

  o more   o less   o about the same

Now, create the Postcard.

• Pick a person in your life who sees you for who you are. Someone who cares about you as you, not as they wish you were.
Choose a postcard. Write a brief message on the card with your
responses to the questions: "Are you living your own authentic
vision of the good life? Why or why not?"

• Send the card to this Repacking Partner. Wait for them to respond; or if you don't hear from them in about a week or so,
call up and see what they think.

CHAPTER 2

Unpacking Your Bags

In the film, *Up in the Air,* the George Clooney character, Ryan Bingham, leads a self-help seminar in which he asks participants to ask themselves the question, "How much does your life weigh?"

He asks them to imagine they are carrying a backpack stuffed with all the stuff they have in their lives. First, the little things — the knick-knacks — and then the bigger stuff, like couches, cars, and home. Afterwards he has his audience move on to the people in their lives — siblings, parents, spouses. All of these go into the imaginary backpack, and Bingham urges participants to feel the weight of this bag and notice how this burden slows them down. He argues that moving is living, and the slower we move, the faster we die. He tells them to rid themselves of the bags' contents and completely free themselves from human connections. We are not like swans, he says, which carry each other symbiotically over a lifetime. Rather, we are sharks, always moving, ever hungry, essentially alone.

This, of course, is where we as authors diverge from Bingham. While the message he begins with sounds in some ways like our own, the big difference is that *Repacking* is not about getting rid of everything and starting over with nothing. Rather, as Richard's experience with Koyie illustrates, it's a matter of systematically considering what we are carrying through life and assessing whether it's helping us get where we want to go or not.

Bingham's initial question is the right one: "How much does your life weigh?" But his solution — *get rid of it all* — is not. And indeed, we discover, in the course of the film, how desperately lonely Ryan Bingham actually is. He has unpacked his bags, but has never learned how to *repack* them. That is the process we will explore now, beginning with unpacking.

Unpacking Your Bags: Choices, Choices, Choices

Ever had the airlines lose your luggage?

You know that laminated card they show you with all the suitcase styles? Ever wonder why there are so many different types of baggage? And so many options for packing things away? Ever wonder what type of person carries this style or that? Or what your own bags say about you?

Go into any luggage store. You'll find briefcases, duffel bags, knapsacks, overnight bags, suitcases with wheels, suitcases with built-in carriers, suitcases with carriers that come off. Fabric choices galore — vinyl, nylon, leather, aluminum, burnished steel, horsehide, alligator, lizard and snake. You can get big, bigger, biggest, small, smaller, and mini, all the way down to tiny little bags that only hold a toothbrush. Whatever you want, wherever you're going, however you're traveling, there's a special bag just for that purpose. When it comes to choosing baggage for a particular journey, the choices are endless.

Of course, the same is true — and to a far greater degree — in our journey through life.

Unfortunately, most of us make our choices quite early on. We come out of school and trade in our bookbag for a brand-new briefcase. We make our choices based on what we see around us and what our needs are at the time. But many people end up carrying this same bag the rest of their lives — long after it has outlived its usefulness.

In this chapter we'll help you take a look at what you're carrying. Does it still fit? Has it gotten a little worn around the edges? Is it time to think about visiting your internal luggage store for something new?

Two main questions to consider: Are the bags that you're carrying still the right ones for where you are going for the rest of your life? And, is your life weighing you down?

The More, the Merrier?

As you begin the process of unpacking and repacking your bags you'll discover a simple truth that you may already know:

You always start out with too much — although you don't know it at the time.

Dave tells a story to illustrate:

When I prepared to hitchhike across Canada, at age eighteen, I thought I had my life pared down to the absolute minimum. Everything I owned fit into my backpack . . . almost. I needed more room for the real essentials: my set of wood flutes, the I-Ching, a brass lockbox that held my ID cards and address book, my journal, my special pen for journal writing, the pouch in which I carried my stash when I had one, my favorite hash pipe, my camera, extra glasses and sunglasses, and the packet of letters from the woman for whose love I was taking this journey in the first place. So I strapped a daypack to the top of the backpack frame, creating a hybrid carrying system that towered over me like a swooping vampire.

Thirty miles north of Toronto, by the side of Canadian Highway #1, I tipped over and couldn't get up. As I struggled to release myself from the belts and buckles that secured my carrying system to me, a pickup truck pulled over and the elderly farmer behind the wheel offered me a ride. He and his younger passenger, who I soon learned was his son, had a good laugh while I fumbled to separate my two packs so as to lift them into the back of the truck. But they were nice enough to let me ride in the cab with them, which turned out to be a godsend, because we hadn't gone five miles before the skies opened up and it began to rain torrentially. Unfortunately it was still pouring when they dropped me off at a roadside rest area half an hour later. I splashed around to the back of the truck and dragged out my backpack. The farmer began to pull away. By the time I noticed, he was twenty yards gone and accelerating — and with him my daypack!

I sprinted down the exit ramp after him, waving my arms and screaming like a crazy person. If someone had been watching, I'm sure they would have taken me for the proverbial ax-wielding hitchhiker, but that didn't stop me. All that mattered at that instant was that my most prized possessions were speeding away from me. The rest of my gear, left soaking in a huge puddle, could have been washed away for all I cared.

As luck would have it, the farmer had to slow for traffic, and I managed to catch up just as he was about to merge onto the highway. He saw my face in his side window and burst out laughing. No doubt I looked hysterical — I was. My vocabulary had been reduced to two words: "Wait!" and "Stop!" but I was getting a lot of mileage out of them, repeating each word in a steady stream at the top of my lungs.

While the farmer and his son slapped their thighs and wiped away tears of laughter, I scrambled back into the rear of the truck and recovered my daypack. I hugged it to my chest with all my might, as if I could squeeze away the terror I'd just experienced. Clutching it like a favorite teddy bear, I plodded back down the ramp towards the rest of my stuff. I'm sorry to say that I didn't even turn back to thank my ride.

Subsequently it has occurred to me that the experience was a pretty good example of how I have too often operated. I've weighed myself down with so much stuff that I haven't been able to enjoy the trip I'm on. Instead of taking care of myself, I spend all my energy taking care of my stuff. And then, typically, in times of transition I pay so much attention to the heavy part of my load that I neglect life's treasures, which then, of course, tend to disappear off into the distance. Only if I'm really lucky — or scream really loud — do I have any chance of ever seeing them again.

The "Packing Principle"

There seems to be a "Peter Principle" when it comes to stuff — whether that stuff fills a knapsack or a lifestyle, whether it's freeze-dried food packages or important responsibilities at work. The "Peter Principle" says that people in an organization rise to their level of incompetence — they keep getting promoted until they end up in a job they can't do effectively.

Most of us, in our lives, accumulate baggage by the same principle. We keep adding things and responsibilities until we get to a point where we can't carry them any more.

It's the "Packing Principle."

What, then, is the solution? There are two parts to it.

First, decide how much you're really willing to carry. And second, decide what goes and what stays.

Ultimately, it comes down to a series of trade-offs. What are you willing to trade in one area of your life to get what you want in another? The unpacking process is a matter of reviewing what you have and considering each item in light of the trade-offs you have to make to keep it.

Probably the most common response we have heard from readers of earlier editions of *Repacking* is the initial reaction they share upon finishing the book. Scores of people have told us how they immediately went to their closets and dressers and began digging through and separating out stuff they no longer felt they needed. Old shoes, forgotten books, broken kitchen appliances go into bags and boxes for second-hand stores or the landfill. We've heard stories from folks who have emptied out shelves — and even rooms — that they'd avoided dealing with for years. This literal lightening of the load is a kind of catharsis for many of us. It's a way of visually comprehending previously unexamined aspects of our lives. And sorting through this stuff is a strategy for jump-starting the deeper process of unpacking and repacking our lives in the metaphorical sense.

Thus, we encourage readers of this edition of *Repacking* — if so moved — to dive into just one closet or dresser before deciding whether to go on an unabashed cleaning binge. But don't stop there. Once we've unpacked the stuff in our lives it's time to unpack our lives themselves.

If you'd like to take a more systematic approach to doing so, you might now turn again to the *Repacking Journal* and complete *The Good Life Checklist*. Alternatively (or having finished it), you might continue wondering about what you really, *really* need in life.

The One Thing I Really, Really, Really Need

In the movie, *The Jerk,* Steve Martin plays an idiot who, through pure dumb luck, strikes it rich by inventing a special handle for eyeglasses. He becomes phenomenally wealthy and indulges himself with a brand-new mansion full of consumer goods. Soon of course, his life goes down the tubes — his personal relationships fall apart, his self-esteem crumbles, and finally, in a classic scene, he staggers through his house, getting ready to leave for good, boasting that he doesn't need anybody or anything. But he can't completely let go. He picks up a chair, an article of clothing, a vacuum cleaner.

"I don't need anything!" he bellows. "Except this . . . and this . . . and this . . . "

By the time he is walking out the front door of his home, he's draped in all kinds of things, with furniture and appliances hanging off every limb. And because it's Steve Martin, he's also got his pants around his ankles.

It's like this for many of us (except for the pants part) as we prepare to unpack and repack. We approach the process thinking "I don't need nothin'," but before we know it, we're groaning beneath the weight of all the things we can't live without. Here, then, is a conversation prompt to get you thinking about the one — and only — thing you really, really, really need. Sharing this with a Repacking Partner will also help you test out whether what you *think* you need is what you *really* need.

Go through your home, mentally or physically, until you've come up with the one thing you really, really, really need. For example, if there were a fire, what item would you grab first? Keep in mind that the "one thing" doesn't necessarily have to be a valuable possession. It might be a treasured photograph, an unpublished novel you're working on, or even your favorite coffee cup.

Ask yourself why this item is so important to you, and see if you can't draw upon this reflection to come up with a principle for why the things that matter to you matter so much. If possible, talk about this with your Repacking Partner and use it as a way to develop some additional guidelines for what you want to continue carrying, and for what you can now leave behind.

Four Reasons for Carrying

When you get right down to it, there are four main reasons why you might be carrying what you're carrying. You can break this down into two scales, and create a matrix to help identify where you stand.

One scale is a continuum between current enjoyment and future payoff. We either do something because we enjoy it, or we expect to get something down the road.

The other scale is a continuum between self and others. We either do something for ourselves, or we do it to help others.

Combining these yields the four categories. So you might be carrying what you're carrying because:

- You enjoy it now for the pleasure it gives you.

- You enjoy it now for the pleasure it gives others.

- You are willing to put up with it now for something it will provide you in the future.

- You are willing to put up with it now for something it will provide others in the future.

An example of the first category might be a job, hobby, or pastime you really love doing. For instance, you may have no problem getting up at 6:00 a.m. on a cold winter day to go skiing.

In the second category, consider something like hosting a party. It might be tons of work for you, but you enjoy it because it's fun for people you care about.

A good example of the third category is physical exercise. You may hate your aerobics class or detest swimming laps, but you do it because you know that afterwards you'll feel better for it.

Into the fourth category falls a lot of people's work. You may not be crazy about your job — you may not even like it at all — but you do it because you have a family to support, or because you want to someday pay for your children's education.

Obviously, in all four of these categories, there's some overlap. For example, you may enjoy some aspects of your job while you're doing them, and put up with others because they may eventually lead to something else. The point of recognizing these categories is not to go through your life and pigeonhole everything you do into one or another. It's simply to help you see that the answer to the question, "Why the #@&%! am I carrying it?" is not that complicated. You can, with a little introspection, develop a pretty clear sense about why you're doing what you're doing — why you're carrying what you're carrying.

And more importantly, this prepares you for doing something about it. It sets you up either to lighten your load, or steel yourself for the burdens you've chosen. Because there are really only two things you can do. You can either keep carrying, or stop carrying.

What most of us do, though, is vacillate. Or whine. If we feel that something's weighing us down — a relationship, a job, the burdens of home ownership — we're usually not willing to just let it go. At the same time, we're often unable to accept the burden as a choice and change our attitude about it. We don't take the time to do what Richard did with the items in his backpack: decide if we really want to be carrying them, and, if the answer is "yes," to carry them as happily as possible.

Human beings have a remarkable ability to persevere if we have a reason for doing so. History is filled with stories of men and women who bore incredible hardships in the name of a cause or a concern they believed in. On the other hand, most of us have a hard time flossing regularly because it hardly seems worth the trouble.

When we unpack and repack, a good deal of what we want to do is simply to decide what's worth the trouble. And then, having decided that something is worth it, own that choice — take responsibility for it — and bear the burden (if it still feels like one) with as much good humor as we can.

The Weight of Success

The more we do, the more responsibilities we have, the heavier our loads tend to be — and the more important it is that we ask ourselves why we're carrying what we're carrying. And yet, it is just when we need most to ask ourselves this question that we find it most difficult. We're too busy, too weighed down by success to stop and reflect.

Ironically, the most important issues in our lives — work, love, place, and purpose — are also usually the most difficult to deal with. And the problems with which we need the most help are the hardest to ask for help with.

All around us, help is available — but we don't avail ourselves of it. Side-by-side on the bookstore shelves, row after row, are books — self-improvement, poetry, autobiography, history, nature — that encourage us to inquire about the meaning of our journey through life. To scratch even the surface of the wisdom contained in these volumes, a person would have to retreat from the world to study full-time. The only way we could ever possibly get these messages about life would be to withdraw from it.

The paradox shouldn't come as a surprise. Life is full of riddles that can only be solved by living them. As Kierkegaard said, "Life can only be understood backwards, but it must be lived forwards."

Often it takes a "wake-up call" of one sort or another — a job loss, the death of someone we love, a significant health challenge — to get us thinking about our problems. And unfortunately, due to the effects of the wake-up call, we're often much less able to deal effectively with the problems than we would be normally.

It's essentially a matter of feeling lost, of not knowing where to go next. Or, as Richard learned recently from a well-respected alpine tour guide named Daniel Sundqvist, of essentially "not knowing which way is up."

Daniel leads hiking and skiing trips in the European Alps for Ryder-Walker Alpine Adventures. When Richard and his wife, Sally, had the privilege of following Daniel's superb leadership through deep snow in the birthplace of skiing, Arlberg, Austria, he filled them in on what to do in the case of an avalanche.

2: Unpacking Your Bags

Virtually no one out-skis an avalanche, he counseled. If you're caught in one, the first thing to do — counter-intuitively — is take off your skis. If you leave them on you'll get anchored in place, and be unable to escape. But once you've abandoned them you're in a position to plan an escape.

As soon as the snow stops moving, said Daniel, you need to confront the inevitable claustrophobia of being buried beneath it. First, create an air space around your mouth, by clearing away the snow and cupping your hands. Then, spit.

Why spit?

Daniel explained: So you know which way is up. You can depend on the law of gravity to tell you which way to start digging. It's not unprecedented for skiers buried in an avalanche to become so disoriented that they actually dig themselves deeper in a fatal attempt to extricate themselves. Had they only employed Daniel's simple trick, they might have survived.

Often, it's such simple steps that make all the difference when, in life, we feel all but buried alive, when we figuratively, if not literally, don't know which way is up.

Many times, we become so wrapped up in the complexity of things that we fail to take the first simple steps that lead to success, or even survival. Letting go of things that weigh us down, making space to breathe, figuring out which way to start digging — these are all simple steps that, when taken, increase our odds of finding our way to a safe place and achieving our goals and objectives.

The evidence is pretty persuasive that most of us — even the most successful of us — will go through periodic "wake-up calls" — when we feel as if we are carrying the weight of the world on our shoulders. Surprisingly, we realize that our world is different than we perceived it. As Rollo May put it in *The Courage to Create*, "Emergence is often experienced by the individual as emergency, with all its attendant stress."[1]

In other words, "wake-up calls" wake us up.

Richard talks about his own series of wake-up calls.

> Many years ago, I thought of myself as a journeyman adult. I had
> come into my own. I was confident. I was settled. I was success-
> ful, comfortable in my way of life. Surprisingly — to me — ev-
> erything skidded to a halt. A series of wake-up calls shifted my
> mental furniture around and permanently rearranged it. First
> one, then a second parent died. I divorced. A work partner died.
> My son left for college. My world caved in. I had to tunnel out.

> My father was only 68, and we never had a chance to say
> good-bye to each other. He was struck by a catastrophic physi-
> cal event — a massive coronary while walking in the skyways
> of downtown St. Paul. Everyone told me that he didn't suffer;
> there wasn't any time. The emergency crew and the doctor who
> happened to be nearby agreed.

> My father disappeared, taking with him my past and his future.
> I was struck by the feeling that by dying so young, he had aged me
> overnight. A new person crawled out, weighted down with heavy
> bags of sadness. I decided I had to repack for my own future.

> Eleven years later my mother died in my arms at 78. We did
> have a chance to say good-bye to each other. With her death, the
> generational curtain was flung open completely. I no longer had
> any protection from the raw edge of total responsibility for my
> life. I had no choice but to unpack and repack.

> After her death I looked in the mirror. I saw a kind of ado-
> lescent in midlife — in some ways no different from what I was
> at 18 — confused and frightened, yet amazed and excited by my
> life. With the same sense of longing for distant places, the same
> wild curiosities and romantic yearnings. I remember exactly
> the same feelings when I was 18. The years between 18 and 49
> seemed now like moments, not decades.

Risking New Ground

Everyone says good-bye to someone or something at various times in their life. It's usually not easy, but the letting go of things is a natural part of life. In order to keep moving forward, occasionally we have to leave things behind.

In order to grow we have to deal with the necessary losses, whatever they are — the death of a loved one, a job layoff, divorce, the loss of property, loss of a dream, seeing our children launched. Personally, we have handled such losses with journaling, introspection, and most importantly, dialogue. They're how we allow the newfound lightness of our load to keep from weighing us down.

In the classic movie, *Dead Poets' Society,* Robin Williams plays professor John Keating, who has returned as a teacher to the prep school he attended as a youngster. He tries to introduce the young men of the school to the joys of English literature, and more importantly, to life. Throughout the film, as they struggle with self-discovery, he challenges them to let their true voices speak.

At one point, he leaps up on his desk. "Why do I stand here?" he asks. He answers his own question: "I stand on my desk to remind myself that we must constantly force ourselves to look at things differently. The world looks different from up here. If you don't believe it, stand up here and try it. All of you. Take turns."

"If you're sure about something," he says as they take turns standing on his desk, "force yourself to think about it another way, even if you know it's wrong or silly. When you read, don't consider only what the author thinks, but take time to consider what you think ... Risk walking new ground."

To risk walking new ground is a challenge we face constantly throughout our lives, and never more poignantly than at midlife. Our interviews, experience, and involvement with people at all stages of

life have led us to believe that nothing is more important to fulfillment than the willingness to "risk walking new ground."

Almost everybody harbors a desire to be something other than
what they have become. Nearly everyone feels compelled to examine
their life and ask, "Why am I carrying all this?"

Our culture has traditionally taught us that shouldering the same
load no matter what the circumstances is more honorable than unpacking our bags and letting go. We hang in there because we are condi-
tioned to believe that we are failures if our relationships or jobs end.

In fact, it may be just the opposite. Making that discovery is what
repacking is all about.

Unpacking Dialogue Questions

In its major forms, unpacking can be one of the most painful of human experiences. At the same time it can be intensely liberating.

How about you? What are you carrying? Are you in a major period of questioning whether to let go of some place, someone, or
something?

Think of a particular situation you're struggling with. Decide
whether it falls under the heading of work, love, place, or purpose.

With that specific situation in mind, reflect on the following
questions and prepare to have a courageous conversation with your
Repacking Partner about them.

- Place: Can I really expect the situation to be any better somewhere else? How?

- Work: Is what bothers me about this job something I would have
  only with this job?

- People: What would it take to "unpack my bags" in this relationship? At what point have I thought enough about my situation —
  at what point is it a mistake to keep "hanging in there"?

- Purpose: Who can I talk with who might help me make more sense of my life?

And one last thing to think about while unpacking:

- What is one thing I really, really don't need to keep?

Unpacking involves looking at both the good and bad in your life — the ugly, too. As you unpack, you'll probably be shocked by some of the baggage that weighs you down. There may not exactly be skeletons in your closets, but chances are there will be at least a few things that have seen much better days.

CHAPTER 3

Repacking Your Place Bag

Do you have a picture of where in the world you belong? A vision of where you would like to live? What are the chances there of being able to do the kind of work you want and earn a suitable income? How do your spouse, partner, and family feel about it? What are their images of where *they* should be?

Many of us have visions of where we would love to live. The purpose of this chapter is to help you focus your vision on where in the world is home. Where is the place you belong? Where do you unpack?

Even if the place in which you're currently living is truly "home" for you, it's a healthy idea to develop a "Plan B": an additional place to consider in the event that circumstances change. It's fun to break the boundaries of your current thinking and at least dream about the other possibilities. If nothing else, doing so can help you appreciate more fully what you have.

A Sense of Place

If you were given the choice, now, to move to anywhere in the world, where would you choose to go? The mountains of Colorado? The high desert in New Mexico? The heart of Paris? Somewhere in the Far East? The bustling center of Rio de Janeiro?

The late naturalist/author Sigurd Olson emphasized our need for a sense of place. He claimed contact with nature is a necessary part of existence:

> It is a long jump from the life of those days to the concentrated civilization of our cities and larger towns, and it is rather hopeless to believe that in the short space of a generation or two, we can completely root out of our system the love of the simple life and the primitive. It is still deeply rooted and it will be hundreds or thousands of years before we lose very much of it.[2]

Richard has personally seen changes come over many people he has guided on wilderness trips. They go, for example, to Africa, to climb a mountain like Kilimanjaro, or to see the great migration of animals. And they come back hooked on sunsets, silence, staring into the fire's coals late at night, sleeping beneath the stars; on touching the basics again.

Most of our lives are no longer tied to the sun, the tides or the changing seasons. We see hunger in the eyes of so many people today, a hunger for contact with the earth . . . a sense of roots, of place. Our sense of place is so tied up with our evolving background and traditions that it simply cannot be ignored. As Sigurd Olson goes on to say, "Wilderness . . . is a spiritual necessity, an antidote to the high pressure of modern life, a means of regaining serenity and equilibrium."

We are rooted physiologically and psychologically to our wild past. Because of the speed of change, we haven't had time to shift gears. As a result, no matter how successful our lives, we can't seem to shake our past. Without some kind of contact with the earth and its simple rhythms, we feel a lack of roots; literally, a lack of *grounding*.

Always Going Somewhere, Never Being Anywhere

Generations of us have grown up under the influences of Hollywood and Madison Avenue. It should come as no great surprise that many see the good life at its best as beautiful people in beautiful places. And what do we do when our own life doesn't match up?

It's easy. We go faster. Or move.

Of course, that doesn't always work in the long run. But who in today's television and computer culture has much to say about the long run?

There never seems to be enough time. We have less for ourselves and far less for each other. We are impatient with people who are reflective or who talk too slowly. We drive fast, make love fast, and expect our Starbucks latte in 15 seconds. A full calendar reflects our importance; time is money. Our weekends are scheduled weeks in advance. We rarely have time for real dialogue or for just "wasting time."

We're more organized but less spontaneous, less alive. We're better prepared for the future, but less able to enjoy the present. We're always going somewhere, never being anywhere. Just where are we going anyway? Where is there?

When will I enjoy my friends? When will I be at home in my home? Will there ever be a time in my life to attend to my family's priorities? It's not just the physical location we're concerned about; it's also the emotional places and spaces we find ourselves in.

Richard met Dan Petersen on one of his African safari treks many years ago. Dan was in the middle of a two-year sabbatical from his orthodontic practice near San Diego. After dental and orthodontic schools, a stint in the Air Force, and 20 years in a joint ortho dontic practice, he says, "I felt I needed to do something different. I was dying from the inside out. My partner and I had created our ideal master plan where we each worked six months and then took six months off. It worked great for 18 years. I had it all except for one thing — inner peace. So I left."

Dan shifted his attention from dental work to spiritual work — with himself. He decided to create new and deeper relationships with "people who are committed to waking up and improving themselves."

For a while, he worked a "comfortable two to three days a week" in his repacked role as holistic orthodontist. During that time, he became a serious student of body/mind psychology, and took inventive new approaches to treating face, jaw and teeth injuries and development problems. He says, "People came to me to consult with them and I always stopped to talk. They couldn't believe the time I spent with them. By keeping my own needs to a minimum I had the time to 'be present' with my patients at a deeper level."

To create a sane oasis for his clients, Dan moved his office to his home overlooking the Pacific Ocean. The office itself reflected Dan's sense of place and his natural way of helping people to heal themselves. The simple, natural setting that looked out through verdant grounds to the ocean rolling in offered a sharp contrast to the stark lights and machinery that keeps most dental patients away from treatment as long as possible.

Dan's clients visibly changed while listening to the ocean and being listened to by Dan. His appreciation for a sense of place made them feel as if they belonged there, too.

As his work deepened, so did Dan, and he began to develop his practice in the direction of personal and leadership coaching. He established *Open Focus,* a practice to coach people in personal and professional transition. He bought property and built a simple, ecologically friendly home in a pristine canyon outside Cortez, Colorado,

People now come to Dan's place to do three to five-day "vision quests," and to receive coaching guidance. He has established the *Sage Canyon Project* to expand and deepen the study of human consciousness, and is attracting friends and colleagues to live and work near him.

As before, Dan's work with people is founded in a deep and abiding sense of a place where he belongs, and in his ability to communicate this sense of belonging to those he works with. His repacking journey will continue, but for now he says, "All this makes me very happy!"

Where in the World Is Home?

Our vision of the good life dictates where we live and how we live. When we acquire a home we also acquire its total environment, including the neighbors, community services, climate, taxes and politics. All of these factors interact with our values, and influence whether or not our home is an inspiring, supportive place that allows us to express the fullness of our being.

We invent and reinvent ourselves again and again during a lifetime. Changing place can be a big part of that, providing a new outlook in more ways than one.

Helen Nearing, in *Loving and Leaving the Good Life*, writes:

> When one door closes, another opens . . . into another room,
> another space, other happenings. There are many doors to open
> and close in our lives. Some we leave ajar, where we hope and
> plan to return. Some doors are slammed shut decisively — "No
> more of that!" Some are closed regretfully, softly — "It was good
> but it is over." Departures entail arrivals somewhere else. Clos-
> ing a door means opening onto new vistas and ventures, new
> possibilities, new incentives. [3]

How about you? Are you ready to close a door? Or are you happy and comfortable where you live now? What are you willing to give up for new vistas, ventures, and views?

If you're considering a new place it's wise to examine what sort of ideal future lifestyle you have in mind, and compare your thoughts with those of your intimates before you go much further.

Otherwise, after moving to a new place, people frequently dis-cover that they haven't really wound up with what they wanted after

all. Conversely, it's not all that uncommon for people to re-conceptu-
alize the place in which they're currently living, or to find something
out about it that they weren't aware of before, so that it seems like a
brand-new place, in which they feel more at home than ever.

    When Dave and his wife, Jennifer, were first married, they had
both of these experiences, as they searched — admittedly in a some-
what haphazard way — for a place to call home. Dave puts it this way:

> Immediately after getting married, Jen and I moved out of the
> apartments we were living in — me in Santa Fe, New Mexico,
> she in Albuquerque — and spent three months, from June to
> early September, house-sitting at the homes of various friends
> and colleagues. It was a rootless existence, but we always felt at
> home wherever we were, mainly because, as newlyweds, we had
> each other. It didn't matter that one week we were living at the
> almost entirely pink-themed house of a woman I worked with,
> taking care of her tiny Pomeranian dog; and the next, we were
> ensconced in a luxurious guest house on the country estate of an
> old friend of Jen's parents. As long as we were with each other,
> that's where we belonged.
>
> At the end of that time we packed up or sold pretty much
> everything we had, and moved to France to pursue our literary
> and artistic dreams. We lived in a tiny apartment on the Left
> Bank in Paris for six months, and then spent late winter and ear-
> ly spring in the south of the country; first in a basically deserted
> tourist village called La Ciotat and then in the artistic communi-
> ty of Aix-en-Provence, where Jen studied painting in the natural
> light made famous by artists like Cezanne and Monet. As exotic
> and unfamiliar as all these places were, they continually felt like
> home, primarily because we both were following our dreams.
> It didn't matter that you could stretch out your arms and touch

both walls in our Paris living room. And who cared that our garret in Aix had only a hotplate to cook on? For us "home" meant a place to write and paint, in spite of whatever it was like.

When our money ran out we moved to Los Angeles, where our best friend was living, and where we knew we'd have work and a roof over our heads. And yet, even though we readily got these things, neither of us, for the entire year or so that we stayed there, ever felt at home. That was primarily because neither of us had a real reason to be there. I had lived in Hollywood a few years earlier and loved it because, at the time, I was trying to break into the movie and television business as a comedy writer. Los Angeles was the place to be for me then, so it was easy to overlook the traffic and crowds and to embrace the Southern California lifestyle. But without the desire to "make it" there, LA was just one vast, faceless megalopolis that we couldn't get out of fast enough.

In fact, it wasn't until we moved — to, of all places, Minneapolis, Minnesota — that we once again felt that we'd arrived where we belonged. And this was surprising in a way, since neither of us had ever lived — or had ever wanted to live — in the Upper Midwest. But because Jen had been accepted to art school there, and I had been hired at a job I really enjoyed, we both immediately felt a connection to the place. We quickly made lots of friends, and discovered a number of places to hang out, hear music and dine; and within a remarkably short time we felt like we'd come home. The sense of belonging we experienced had as much to do with what we were doing as where we were doing it. This isn't to say that the physical and cultural aspects of our city were superfluous; rather, it's just to note how much our feelings of connection to a place depend on feeling connected to ourselves.

Finally, after four years in the Twin Cities, we came out west
to Seattle, where we've now lived for going on two decades.
Having bought a house and had a child, our roots are sunk much
more deeply than they were in all the places we lived in the early
years of our marriage. But even so, the sense of belonging to a
place, the feeling that where we are is where we were meant to
be, still depends just as much — if not more — on our attitude
about the place as it does on the place itself. When you have a
good reason for being where you are and know what it is and
why you are there, then it begins to feel like home remarkably
quickly. But if those elements are lacking, even the most beautiful and exciting of places never feel entirely welcoming.

Listening Point

Sigurd Olson, in his book, *Listening Point,* writes:

> I named this place Listening Point because only when one comes
> to listen, only when one is aware and still, can things be seen
> and heard. Everyone has a listening point somewhere.[4]

Where is your listening point? Where are your places of quiet
where the universe can be contemplated with awe?

Larry Christie, one of the more successful and fulfilled financial
planners in the country, leaves for his listening point at noon every
Friday. The five-hour drive to his log cabin on Tait Lake, in northern
Minnesota, has become a listening point in itself. During the drive he
listens to tapes of poetry and classic literature on his car stereo. Larry
says of his cabin, "It's my spiritual refuge, where the good life prevails.
My wife Jean and I consider it 'home.' We read, journal, listen to clas-
sical music and take long walks with our dog.

"I really love my life now, being in my 70s," he says. "I feel like
I've spent a lot of time planting; now I'm harvesting. Today love and

place get more of my attention than work. I'm putting less pressure on myself. I know I'll never retire, but I'll downshift soon to working only three days a week so that I can spend even more quiet time at the cabin. It's the place that really opens my soul."

One of Richard's listening points was his 110-year-old log cabin on the edge of the Chequamegon National Forest, an area of over a million acres of forest, lakes, and rivers that make up northwestern Wisconsin's "Great Divide" country. Richard comments, "When I was up there, my pace was slow and deliberate, like that of the seasons around me. I didn't have a telephone, or even electricity. The evenings were warmed by the romantic shadows of the woodstove and kerosene lamps. For years I used this cabin as one of my listening points for writing and renewal. These days, I've captured that same feeling in my home on the St. Croix River. Even though it has a few more 'creature comforts,' it still affords me the opportunity to tap into that slower rhythm. I can move into the feel of the river, which carries me along at its own steady pace. I'm able to see the gentle flow of the water, hear the wind through the trees, and at the same time, hear myself too."

At different times in our lives, we all yearn for a listening point — a place to unpack and be fully ourselves — but few act on that yearning. One who did stop to listen to the sound of a different drummer was Henry Thoreau. He explained his reasons for living alone in the woods by Walden Pond:

> I went to the woods because I wished to live deliberately, to
> front only the essential facts of life, and see if I could not learn
> what it had to teach, and not, when I came to die, discover that I
> had not lived.[5]

Richard admits that his motivations are similar. "There are many times," he says, "when I finish my writing, don my walking shoes and hike off into the woods. Sometimes my walk is interrupted by a deer or wild turkey shuffling down the path. On these walks, it often strikes me that the most alive people I know all take some time to be quiet. They know how to be present in most situations in which they find themselves, because they take time to listen to themselves."

In 1933, Admiral Richard E. Byrd decided to spend the seven dark months of the Antarctic winter alone at a weather station deep in the continent's interior. "I wanted to sink roots into some replenishing philosophy," he said. He discovered "the sheer excitement of silence." During that time, he wrote, "There were moments when I felt more alive than at any other time in my life." Byrd realized that "half the confusion in the world comes from not knowing how little we need."

Of course, you don't have to seclude yourself away in the Antarctic to hear the sounds of silence. Dave finds his listening point in the heart of the city. "On summer nights especially, I like to get on my bike and tool around the city. I feel an incredible sense of freedom in being able to observe life all around me, but at the same time, I'm not trapped in traffic or on crowded sidewalks or in smoky bars. I listen to the sound of the wind rushing around my helmet, mingled with snatches of conversations I catch as I ride past. The ongoing collage of images sweeping past my field of vision expands my mind. I get my best creative work done alone in the night air, just me and my bicycle, and those half-million stories in the naked city swirling about me."

Listening Point Postcard Exercise

Having spent — or at least thought about — spending time alone in your listening point, it's worthwhile to consider who you might include on another visit. Here's a brief postcard exercise to help you do that.

Where is your listening point?

Imagine that you can travel to any "listening point" in the world for a weekend to consult a wise person about the good life.

Directions

- On the front of the postcard, create or clip an image of the place you'd travel to for writing and reflection — a place where you can contemplate the big picture of your life: a "listening point."

- On the back of the postcard, write some big life questions on which you'd like a wise person's counsel.

- Address the postcard to the person whose counsel you'd most like. This person can be known or unknown to you, living or dead, famous or infamous.

- Send the postcard to your Repacking Partner and discuss your "listening point" with them. Where is it? How often do you go there? What life questions do you reflect on, and how?

CHAPTER 4

Repacking Your Relationship Bag

We Are All Hadza

In decades of regular "inventure" treks to Tanzania, Richard has had numerous opportunities to live, work, and play with the Hadza, one of the last hunter-gatherer peoples still extant on the planet. The Hadza live essentially as they have for tens of thousands of years, in kin groups of several dozen, hunting and gathering food from their environment. It has been, for time immemorial, a completely sustainable lifestyle, one in which every person has a role and purpose and is supported by the entire group of which they are a part. When Richard and his fellow "inventurers" spend time with the Hadza, they inevitably feel a sense of "coming home" to a way of life that seems remarkably familiar, in spite of how different it is from how we in the contemporary world live our lives.

But, of course, that's really no surprise. The way the Hadza live is how human beings survived together for almost all of our common history. The bonds they share amongst each other are, to a great extent, "hard-wired" into us. We are built, in other words, to form deep and abiding relationships among those close to us that enable us to survive and thrive together in the world. We are defined to a much greater extent than we tend to acknowledge in our busy, 21st century lives, by our "tribe."

Thus, when we consider our definition of the good life: "living in the place I belong, *with people I love,* doing the right work, on purpose," it makes perfect sense, both individually, and in tune with our collective identity, that the relationship component — *people I love* — is so key to our sense of happiness and fulfillment. We need, to put it simply, our "tribe" in order to feel whole and wholly alive.

The following story illustrates what we mean:

We are a dozen men "of a certain age" on an "Inventure Trek" in Africa led by Richard and his long-time trekking partner, Daudi Peterson. One evening at our camp in northern Tanzania, about 50 kilometers from the Olduvai Gorge where Louis and Mary Leakey made their breakthrough discoveries of hominid evolution, we are joined by a group of about ten Hadza elders. We are all amazed by one in particular, a spry and leathery little elf of a man, named Kampala. He is the oldest and arguably the wisest of the Hadza, pegged by his peers at somewhere between 94 and 98 years of age. He claims that his age doesn't seem that special to him, although he does admit to being surprised at times that he is "still here."

We are offered a demonstration of how the Hadza harvest honey from a beehive in a baobab tree, and when the youngster doing the harvesting, Mwapo, throws the honeycomb down from the upper branches to the ground, Kampala is across the grass in a split second to claim his first share. Unabashed in his appetite and desires, Kampala has us all in stitches at his sheer vitality and aliveness.

Later, after nightfall, we receive a vivid illustration of his role among his people and the degree to which his wisdom pervades their shared experience. Kampala, through Daudi as translator, shares with us a long and rambling but endlessly compelling version of the Hadza creation story, a dramatic and complex tale of a young girl, her warrior suitor, and her man-eating giant of a father. The younger Hadza men listening to him have the same rapt look of attention that we have seen in our own children as they watch a Spielberg movie. The details he shares are rich, but in many ways, secondary.

At one point, one of the other elders, Philipo, a man of about 70, interrupts to correct Kampala on a point of fact regarding one of the animals in the story, the black mamba snake. "The black mamba's tongue is not purple, it's blue," he says. Kampala shoots back, "Blue, purple, what's the difference? I'm telling a story here, and purple works for the story!" The Hadza, young and old, erupt in laughter, and once the interaction is translated for us, we do, too.

After completing his culture's creation story, Kampala asks that we share ours. Our group, which fortunately includes a physicist, cobbles together a version of the Big Bang and Darwinian evolutionary theory. We make the point that in our creation story, the tribes of the Olduvai Gorge, including the Hadza, are the first people. We all come from the Hadza, and, therefore, in a very real way, are all, at our essence, Hadza, too.

At this, there is a flurry of conversation among Kampala and his fellow hunter-gatherers. We ask Daudi what is being discussed, and eventually it comes out. It turns out that the Hadza are talking about a different creation story they have than the one that Kampala shared with us. It is told only to their own people; rarely, if ever, shared with outsiders. And it begins, Daudi tells us, "In the beginning, the Hadza were baboons . . ." We are humbled to be made privy to this unique evolutionary story that the Hadza are aware of. This genuine moment of cross-cultural connection floors us all, Westerner and African alike, and leads, in a while, to the Hadza men sharing with us a number of their traditional songs, hauntingly beautiful call-and-response melodies, similar in some ways to Southern spirituals we have heard, a few with dance accompaniment that Kampala leads in.

Afterwards Kampala asks our group to sing a few of our own traditional songs. We offer up "If I Had a Hammer" and "This Little Light of Mine." When he asks for one with a dance, we scratch our heads a bit, but then eventually settle on the only such tune we all know, the "Hokey-Pokey." Tentatively, but with increasing verve, we begin, "You put your left leg in, you take your left leg out, you put your left leg in and you shake it all about. You do the hokey-pokey and you turn yourself around, that's what it's all about."

And this, then you have to picture: Some 20 or so men around a campfire in Africa, Americans, Europeans, and Hadza alike, all dancing together doing the hokey-pokey. Kampala rises and joins us, and when we get to the final verse, "You put your whole self in," leaps in and out with the rest of us, crying "Nzuri sana! (Very fine!)"

And it seems in this moment that it is all there: the authenticity and wholeheartedness, exactly what we have all come to Africa to experience, however fleetingly.

You put your whole self in; that's what it's all about.

It was easy for us on the trek to define our "tribe" at that moment. The connections we felt among our group and with our Hadza hosts made the bonds between us self-evident. We "put our whole selves in," easily and naturally, without holding back. It was obvious to all of us that "that's what it's all about."

Of course, it's much harder, most of the time, to identify and commit to our "tribe." Most of us live among intertwining communities at work, in our neighborhoods, and with our families. The good news about this, though, is that it allows us to form deep and meaningful bonds with a number of different "tribes," even if these tribes are quite small — like just you and a life partner.

It's just a matter of "putting our whole selves in."

Traveling Together

One of the challenges along the way to a successful long-term relationship with someone is making it through the "travel test." You've been seeing another person for a while and you come to the point where you decide to take a trip together. Discussing the event afterwards with your closest friend you'll say one of two things.

Either, "It was great, thank heavens. At least we can travel together."
Or, "It was a nightmare. It's over — we can't even travel together."

Traveling with someone is a great way to get to know them — or wish you didn't. Little faults and foibles are magnified. Simple choices about where to eat, what to wear, how to spend the evening, turn into major life decisions. If you can navigate through these decisions with your fellow traveler, you'll feel closer, more connected. If you can't, you'll want to go home on the next plane out.

It's the same thing, if not so obvious, as you journey through life with someone. Your ability to make decisions, solve problems, and in general, travel together successfully, has a lot to do with how enjoyable you'll find the trip.

Fortunately — or perhaps unfortunately — most people, when the going gets tough, don't feel they can send their travel partners packing. A few feel inclined to take a hike themselves, but even this is not usually considered an option.

Too often, we just trudge along together with our partner, unable or unwilling to improve things, hoping in the back of our minds that something or someone better will come along and bring us the romance and adventure we feel we're missing.

If the success of online dating sites is any gauge, millions and millions of people are longing for a soulmate who'll sweep into their lives and sweep them away emotionally. But how many of those millions are willing to cast free their emotional moorings in order to experience the highest heights of passion? How many are willing to let themselves be fully seen by another person? How many are willing, as we put it, to fully unpack?

Apparently, millions of us are looking for relationships in which all parties involved have their bags fully unpacked. But many of us are too afraid, or too tired, or who-knows-what to let other people see what we're carrying. In the end we want the overwhelming ecstasy of a once-in-many-lifetimes love relationship, without the messiness and pain that goes along with creating one.

This is perfectly understandable — if not very realistic.

The simple (though incredibly hard to accept) truth is this: in order to have an intense, meaningful, fully alive, and exciting relationship with another person, we have to be willing to unpack our bags. Unfortunately, no Prince Charming is going to ride up and sweep us off our feet to live happily ever after. No beautiful, wealthy models from *People* magazine are going to appear and whisk us away to their cottage on the beach.

In order to experience our fantasies, we have to create them.

In order to have the kinds of friendships and love relationships we dream of, we have to be the kind of friend and lover that other people dream of as well.

The first step, then, is to get clear about just who we are in our relationships.

Choosing Your Fellow Travelers

Dave says, "When I was in junior high, I came home crying almost every day. There was this group of kids that used to torment me. One day they'd gang up on me in a snowball fight. The next, they'd steal my homework. Another time they'd hold me down and take turns spitting on me.

"Finally, my mom asked me why I kept hanging around with them if they made me so unhappy.

"'Mom, I have to!' I cried. 'They're my FRIENDS!'

"It wasn't until years later, when I actually met some people who liked me for who I was, that I realized those junior high kids weren't really my friends.

"On the other hand, maybe they were, because they taught me a valuable lesson — not everyone is my friend. And more importantly, I don't have to hang around with people who aren't."

As you consider your own life and the people with whom you are surrounded, ask yourself "How many are my friends?" How many of them are what we call "nutritious people"?

Nutritious people are the people in our life who genuinely "feed" our souls. Who nurture the deepest parts of us that need nurturing. They are the good listeners who truly hear what we have to say. Who reflect back to us our innermost thoughts and feelings. Who listen without judging. Whose eyes light up when they see us and whose presence lightens our mood, too.

The most nutritious people for us are those that love us with the fewest plans for our improvement, and that allow us to love them back completely. Such relationships need not (and as often as not, don't) involve even the slightest hint of sexual or physical intimacy. They are, instead, the close relationships that make us feel seen and heard for who we are; the friends and family members with whom we feel we were meant to travel through life.

The Three Journeys of Intimacy

What we are looking for in our relationships with nutritious people is, quite simply, intimacy. As human beings in the early 21st century, we have a powerful hunger for meaningful connections with other people, but an almost pathological inability to make them. Many of us don't even know what intimacy means.

Psychologist and author Marilyn Mason defines intimacy as "being connected and close through shared contact in a variety of activities that are informal, deep, and personal."[6] She says that it is a process, not static, but active and recurring.

In other words, intimacy is a journey.

With that in mind, we have identified three types of journeys we typically take along the road to greater intimacy with another person. These aren't necessarily sequential, nor do you have to cross each one off to achieve a deeper level of intimacy.

As Marilyn Mason said, intimacy is a process. As such, it continues to evolve throughout our lives. Each of the three journeys evolve along with us. Nevertheless, you may find it useful to consider them as a means of seeing whether you are on the right road at the right time with the people in your life about whom you care — or want to care — most.

The three journeys are:

- Day Trips

- Weekend Getaways

- Lifetime Journey

As you read about each of these, make a note of where you are with your fellow travelers. Are you on the right journey with the people you want to be with? If not, why not? If so, how can you make the journey even better?

Day Trips

Intimacy begins with a toe in the water. When we first meet someone with whom we feel a kinship, we usually approach cautiously, with great anticipation, walking on eggshells. Human beings are funny this way. The more we like someone, the less we're willing to let on. Unlike our friends in the animal kingdom, who proudly display feathers or other finery to demonstrate their attractions, we often veil our best qualities when we feel an affinity — particularly an initial affinity — for someone else.

You've seen this phenomenon at high school dances; you've probably participated in it yourself. The young people most attracted to each other are those least likely to get together. Teenagers find it much easier to talk to someone who's just "a friend," than someone with whom they might conceivably be romantically inclined. As adults, looking back on this, it's charming — we laugh at how silly and scared we were at the time.

But what's charming at 16 or 17 is downright depressing at 40 or 45 — and yet many, if not most of us, continue to make the same mistake no matter how old we get. What's pathetic is that we make this mistake — not with a stranger we spy across the dance floor — but with the people in our lives we know and love best.

Think about it. How much easier is it to open up to a stranger on a plane or in a bar than to your "significant other" or close business associates? When was the last time you let someone close to you get *really* close to you?

Many of us treat our close relationships as if we're merely on a "day trip" with the person or persons involved. The continuation of the voyage is contingent on the success of each day. If things don't go well, we're gone — if not literally, at least from an emotional standpoint. Metaphorically, if not literally, our bags are packed for a quick exit at the first sign of trouble.

You know what this is like. You come home from a party with your longtime partner. It's been a trying evening and you're both worn out. Somebody says something and before you know it, you're embroiled in the mother of all arguments, and accusations are flying faster than either of you can make them up. Soon, you're wondering why you ever got involved with this person in the first place — thinking how much richer and more exciting your life would be if only you were alone.

Why is it that even our deepest relationships are on such fragile ground? Why does it seem that even the people we're closest to are only a step away from being on the other side of the planet? Isn't it odd that two people who can converse all day long, every day, for months, even years on end, can be only a few ill-chosen words away from never wanting to speak to each other again?

And yet this is the human condition. So if we're serious about moving forward in any significant way, this is where we've got to unpack our bags. In order to think at all of establishing and sustaining meaningful long-term relationships with our loved ones, we've got to begin at the beginning.

And at this beginning lies what we call the concept of a Day Trip. How do you truly travel with someone else for the course of one day? And how do you unpack and repack to do so?

One Day at a Time

You know how it is when you're first getting to know someone you like — they can do no wrong. All their little quirks are charming. The way they hold a knife, their choice in music, the way they drive a car, it all seems inspired. You can't get enough of them and want to see more.

Eventually, as you get to know each other better, your appreciation for some of their characteristics may deepen. Knowing the story of why they cut all their meat before eating it, for example, may make you more accepting of their need to do so. On the other hand, familiarity may breed contempt.

So what has changed? Not them, but you.

This means that if you want to re-acquaint yourself with the person you once cared so much for, you can. Taking a Day Trip is an easy way to begin.

Similarly, if you're just getting to know someone and are uncertain about how far you want to travel with them, the Day Trip is a good place to start.

Day Trip Itinerary

When we talk about the Day Trip, we're not just referring to a concept. We're also talking about an actual journey, complete with places to go, sights to see, things to do, and things to learn about each other along the way. The basic idea of the Day Trip is pretty straightforward. Packing for the Day Trip means considering what aspects of yourself and your partner you'd like to deal with over the course of an eight-hour day.

To develop your Day Trip itinerary, ask yourself the following questions.

- If you had just eight hours to spend with someone, with WHOM would it be?

- In what PLACE would it be?

- What would you DO?

Create a real itinerary for your Day Trip. Consider the places you'd like to go, the issues you'd like to discuss, the things you'd like to do. Make it an "official" itinerary, with times and everything. Then do it! Take the Day Trip.

Weekend Getaways

This is the journey of intimacy on which most people find them-selves, even with the people to whom they are closest. The level of commitment we feel is about what you would expect in a situation where you knew you had to spend a weekend with someone. We're willing to "make nice" or "get along" over certain things, but since we tend to be operating under the assumption that "this too shall pass," we're typically unwilling to make any substantive changes in our own behavior or in the situation itself to make things better.

On a weekend trek, you have plenty of time to share ideas. Hopes, dreams, plans for the future — they all trip easily off the tongue. In 48 or 72 hours with someone, you can get to know them really well; you can talk about pretty much everything.

But it's still talk. Over the course of a weekend you can discuss your hopes and dreams, but you can't see them realized. You can make plans for the future, but you can't implement them. There's a certain theoretical or dream-like quality to all your interactions. It's like summer camp: things can get fairly intense, but there's a built-in end point or escape hatch that makes everything just slightly unreal.

This is the essence of what we mean when we talk about "a bag by the door." Many of us — even in our closest relationships — are packed and ready to leave. Even though we're present physically, we've still got a bag, partially packed, by the door. We're feel like we're just one Facebook message away from a long-lost love, one chance meeting with a mysterious stranger; a winning lottery ticket away from picking up our bag and heading out. This is easily under-standable and makes perfect sense, given human nature. Historically, in order to survive we've needed to be highly flexible and adaptable, and readily willing to attach ourselves to the next stronger, better-looking, or smarter king or queen who came along.

But does this serve us nowadays? How much richer and more fulfilling would our relationships be if we were more fully committed to them? What would it be like if the "bag by the door" were unpacked and put away? How, in other words, can we "fully unpack" with another?

The concept of the Weekend Getaway provides you with a means to consider this question. Because ultimately, what we pack in the "bag by the door" is the same as what we pack for the Weekend Getaway. Thus, examining the "whats" and "whys" of our Weekend Getaway bag enables us to look more clearly into what matters most to us. We get a better sense of what we couldn't live without, what means most to us, and what most clearly defines for ourselves who and what we are.

In dozens of popular films, a day or two is all it takes for a couple of people to have their lives completely turned upside-down. Strangers meet, bond over some unexpected occurrence, and, as a result, come to a completely new perspective on each other and ultimately themselves. Typically there are laughs and tears along the way, and plenty of misunderstandings, but the eventual result is that both characters have a sort of epiphany in which their understanding for and appreciation of each other grows immensely. In just a few days, or even, in some cases, a few hours, they become, in the complete sense of the term, soulmates. Despite starting out distant from one another emotionally, and even geographically, they end up forming a real bond, one that is deep, abiding, and certain to last through a sequel or two.

The good news is — as is said about successful Hollywood films — this Weekend Getaway "has legs." Hollywood can do it, and you can, too. The Weekend Getaway concept can help you to establish, re-establish, and maintain deeper relationships with friends, family, and co-workers.

Weekend Getaway Itinerary

Like the Day Trip, the Weekend Getaway is first and foremost, an inward journey. Although you may want to take an actual getaway with your Weekend Getaway partner, it's not essential that you go away and sequester yourselves somewhere to experience it. Nor do you have to take two whole days to get any value from it (although it's rarely a bad idea to get away for a while).

To develop your Weekend Getaway itinerary, ask yourself the following questions.

- If you had just 48 hours to spend with someone, with WHOM would it be?

- In what PLACE would it be?

- What would you DO?

Create a real itinerary for your Weekend Getaway. Write down the places you'd like to go, the issues you'd like to discuss, the things you'd like to do. Make it an "official" itinerary, with times and everything. Then do it! Take the Weekend Getaway.

Lifetime Journey

Whenever we read in the newspaper about a couple who are celebrating their 50th wedding anniversary, we tend to experience a mixture of both sentimentality and awe. It seems sweet that the pair has stayed together for so long, but at the same time we're aghast that any two people could put up with each other for half a century. How have they weathered the changes? Have they managed to grow? Do they still love each other?

There's certainly plenty of room for debate about whether human beings are "meant" to form life-long bonds through marriage or other social contracts. Certainly it's not the lifestyle for everyone. But at some level, it's what we're all looking for. People want that ongoing, never-ending intimacy. We all want to live happily ever after till death do us part.

How, then, is this sort of lifetime journey possible with someone else, especially given the transient nature of today's society and the quickly changing needs and expectations of contemporary adults?

Peter Russell says that relationships are contemporary western society's "yoga." Yoga, in this case, is used in its original sense, to mean "union," especially spiritual union. Russell's point is that we can — and should — use our interpersonal relationships as a form of meditative yoga to improve ourselves and society.[7]

Most of us are most familiar with yoga as physical practice that enhances strength and flexibility. And indeed, we need to nurture both these qualities — mentally and emotionally, as opposed to merely physically — in order to successfully carry on a lifetime journey with another. But historically, yoga is about liberation, from the endless cycle of death and rebirth, ultimately, but, as a practical matter, from the fluctuations of the mind that continually distract us from seeing the essential core of our true being.

If we think of our deepest personal relationships in this way, as a means to more clearly reveal to ourselves who we really are, then it's likely we'll be more apt to hang in there for the long haul. This doesn't mean, of course, that there aren't occasions and situations that can be toxic and from which the only recourse is to extract ourselves, but it does suggest that it's in our best interest to recognize that sometimes what we're experiencing during difficult times are merely those mental and emotional fluctuations, and not an authentic expression of our deepest selves. And that awareness can, perhaps, enable us to carry on together for the lifetime journey.

Conceiving of our interpersonal relationships in terms of a lifetime journey, therefore, may be a particularly effective type of "relationship yoga." Imagine how things would be if — instead of clinging to the vague notion that somewhere out there, there was someone better for us — we were willing to unpack for an ongoing journey, no matter how long or how far it may take us. Supposedly this is the idea behind traditional marriage, but in practice these days it works out only about half the time. And even in marriages that do stay together, it's often because the parties involved have totally checked out. They're living together, but are farther apart than many couples who have had the courage to face up to the differences and separate.

Thus, the Lifetime Journey doesn't, by definition, require that the parties involved remain in absolute proximity to one another. Successful lifetime journeys can be carried out by people who live miles, even continents, apart. Because the lifetime journey involves a change of perspective as opposed to a change of location, one needn't rush off to some distant location in order to maintain the connection. We're talking about the "long haul" here, so it's only natural that there are times when you and those with whom you are on a lifetime journey are not together.

Nietzsche called marriage a "grand dialogue." In order to sustain that dialogue, partners in any long-term relationship must engage in an ongoing "courageous conversation." They must be willing to share their innermost thoughts and feelings in the most radical sense — facing their fears and honoring their differences together.

Too often, people end up tied together instead of moving along the same path. Their ideas about what constitutes the good life are not in alignment, so they're continually tripping over each other. Instead of supporting one another on the journey, they're just getting in each other's way.

The challenge, of course, is to figure out the delicate dance that allows each person a full expression of his or her essential humanity and true nature. And this typically requires that most elusive of feelings for one another: unconditional love. It's hard enough to grant this feeling to even ourselves; how much more difficult it is to offer such grace to another!

And yet, perhaps surprisingly, many of us regularly practice this sort of full-on emotional openness with and support for another being in our lives: our pets. In some cases, the clearest example of a lifetime journey a person experiences is the unconditional love they feel toward a dog or cat. In which case, it may not be for their lifetime the journey lasts, but only as long as Fluffy or Rex is around. Even so, this shorter version of the lifetime journey can provide a model for something fuller and more complete. Think of it as a map to help prepare a Lifetime Journey Itinerary.

Lifetime Journey Itinerary

The itinerary for a Lifetime Journey becomes a reflection of your deepest feelings about yourself, your journey partner, and how you see your long-term connection ultimately unfolding. Generally, the itinerary for a lifetime journey is less strict than for the shorter trips. It's apt to be described in terms of purpose and direction as opposed to destination.

Still, it's useful to engage in the same sort of dialogue for the lifetime journey as you did for the other two. It's also not a bad idea to regularly repeat this exercise to see if you're still tracking along with your lifetime journey partners.

The question comes up again and again: Are you still traveling together? If so, how can you continue to do so? If not, how can you get back on track? Ask yourself:

- If you could spend the rest of your life with just one other person, with WHOM would it be?
- In what PLACE would it be?
- What would you DO?

Create a real itinerary for your Lifetime Journey. Write down the places you'd like to go, the issues you'd like to discuss, the things you'd like to do. Make it an "official" itinerary, with times and everything. Then, do it! Take the Lifetime Journey.

Finding Your Repacking Partners

In the earlier editions of *Repacking,* we made two assumptions that turned out to be inaccurate for many of our readers. First, we assumed that really the sole consideration when it came to relationships for most people had to do with finding their life partner or "soulmate." And second, we mistakenly figured that those focused on doing so had been successful — that they were already in a deep and meaningful relationship with someone they cared deeply about.

As it turns out, what more and more people are hungry for isn't necessarily a connection to one other person; rather, we hear more typically that folks are missing out on a sense of belonging to a group of people that share similar hopes and dreams or a sense of purpose in life. What lots of people are seeking, in other words, is a "crew," or, to put it in anthropological terms, a kin group of sorts, or a small tribe. Again, it's a harkening back to our hunter-gatherer roots. We're biologically adapted, if you will, to a sense of connection with a band of several dozen or so that are pursuing a common goal.

In his groundbreaking *Bowling Alone: The Collapse and Revival of American Community,* Robert Putnam draws on research done with more than half a million people to show how people today have become increasingly disconnected from family, friends, and neighbors. He argues that the solution for this sense of disconnectedness is to invest in "social capital"; in other words, to come together with others to work together for the common good, even in small ways like having neighborhood picnics, or, as is suggested by his title, sharing recreational activities like participation in bowling leagues.

What we've heard from our readers accords neatly with Putnam's observations and advice. And the antidote to this sense of disconnectedness comes back, we believe, to our definition of the good life. The relationship component refers to "the people I love." Consequently, living the good life doesn't depend on finding that one special person, but on revealing ourselves and connecting with whoever we are close to. Many of us naturally think that the only person we could possibly connect with at this deepest level would have to be a romantic partner, but that's not the case. Self-disclosure — the healthy unpacking that reveals who you are to another person — is often most easily done with people who are "just friends." Very few of us have absolutely *no one* to talk to, so we needn't feel left out if we don't currently have a significant other.

Also, it's been our experience that unpacking with friends or associates has the effect of drawing other people into our lives. We've seen it again and again: when people repack and begin living the good life as they see it, they seem to exude a certain quality that makes meeting people easier, more natural, and more frequent.

The more we're able to reveal our true selves to others and the more completely we're able to affirm those connections, the more likely we are to sustain the abiding unity for which we are designed.

It's the antithesis of what many of us do, which is to hold ourselves at arms' length, to metaphorically (or even literally) keep a bag packed by the door. Secretly — or not so secretly — we're waiting for someone better. And should he or she appear, we're ready to go.

We've all seen it: a friend who takes his wedding ring off for trips out of town; another who complains and complains about her husband, but never talks to him about what she feels; couples who see "separate vacations" as the solution to all their problems, real or imagined.

Of course these are the very attitudes and actions that keep people from forming the kinds of relationships for which they yearn. The things we do for love are often the very things that keep us from experiencing it. This is ironic, because most of our actions are driven, in one way or another, by that vital need to connect with someone else in a deep and significant way.

A friend of ours complained that he felt unable to really open up to his wife because she did not have a "rich inner life" like his. Paradoxically, it was his inability to open up that kept him from seeing his wife's deeper inner life. What he wanted to say to her most is what he feared most to put into words.

These types of cycles feed on each other. Relationships fall into patterns from which neither party seems able to escape. In the extreme these patterns become pathological. But for most of us they just take the form of habit, unspoken expectation, and slowly-but-surely-eroded trust.

Admittedly it's not always like this, but it happens all too often. Look around — or within — and you'll find a deep well of despair in the area of human relationships. Here's an arena in which our hopes and dreams exceed our capabilities. We have the ability to experience these overwhelming emotions, but not the skill to manage them. It's as if we've got the keys to emotional Ferraris, but never learned to drive. Is it any wonder so many of us crash and burn?

If you were to put every one of our motivations — to make money, become famous, conquer the world, whatever — into a big pot and boil them down, they'd all reveal the same essence — we want to be loved. It's trite, but true. All our jumping about, all our inventing, everything from our first words to our last dying gasp has that same single source.

So we keep packing more and more into our lives, all in a desperate attempt to get friends, families, even perfect strangers to love us. Ironically, we need to do just the opposite.

We need to unpack.

We need to open our hearts and minds, and put into words our innermost thoughts, feelings, hopes, dreams, desires. Only by over-coming our fear of exposure can we truly be seen.

How Do We Fully Unpack?

Sidney Jourard, in his classic book, *The Transparent Self*, predicted that people who love deeply would live longer. His theory was that if we revealed ourselves to each other, we would live healthier, more vital lives, with less disease, less dis-ease.[8]

Jourard's hypothesis has been validated by many longitudinal studies. George Vaillant studied a large group of male Harvard alumni over more than 40 years following their graduations from college. Part of the research was designed to determine what factors separated the healthy grads from the unhealthy ones. Who had become diseased or disabled; who had died?

Vaillant disclosed the startling findings in his book, *Adaptation to Life*. It turned out that neither diet, nor exercise, nor overall fitness was the critical factor — the single most important key to health and well-being was self-disclosure.[9]

Individuals in Vaillant's healthy group reported the presence in their lives of at least one "nutritious" person — someone with whom they could consistently share their thoughts and feelings openly. For some, it was their spouse, for others (even married), it was a friend or work colleague.

The most common reasons we hear for people "keeping a bag by the door," include:

- "She's not interested in what I care about."

- "He just doesn't get it. And he's not interested in listening to me."

- "She's too busy — there's no time."

- "I feel invisible around him."

Sidney Jourard claims that each of us has within ourselves the potential for "courageous conversation"— self-disclosure — hundreds of times every day. He supports, as does Vaillant, the benefits of fully unpacking our emotional bags on a regular basis.

All relationships with others mirror our relationship with ourselves. Feelings that are "buried alive" rise from the grave to haunt us with illness and dis-ease. Developing better relationships with friends and loved ones means developing a better relationship with ourselves.

When we keep our emotional bags packed, we lose touch with others and ourselves.

In order to unpack with others, we need to start at square one — unpacking our own bags. So how do you do it? How do you fully unpack?

The Fully Unpacked Relationship

Earlier we discussed how different people tend to focus on different aspects of the good life in different ways and at different times in their lives. Some tend to be preoccupied with Work — the "what?" question. Others turn their attention to Place — the "where?" question. Still others tend to be focused on People — the "who?" question. And again, we're all likely to find ourselves concentrating more on different good life components at different times in our lives.

So, just because when you were in your thirties, you were highly directed along the Work path, doesn't mean there won't come a time later in life when concerns about Place or People take precedence. This awareness has a lot to do with living the good life for your whole life.

It also has a lot to do with developing and sustaining long-term, "fully-unpacked" relationships. In order to really connect with another person, we need to understand and embody transparency. We need to be able to disclose our innermost secrets and reveal our true selves. We need to be willing to see other people for who they are, too. And this means having the courage to not only speak our truths, but to listen, as well.

Being "fully unpacked" with another person means you both are unpacked. If either of you still has a "bag by the door," then something's not right. Most people, when they're less than completely satisfied in a relationship — whether it's a romance, a friendship, even a business association — think that if only they could get the other person to reveal a little bit more about themselves, then everything would work out. In fact, the only trick — and it's not really a trick at all — to deeper, more meaningful relationships, is to reveal *yourself*. The more you can let someone else in, the more they'll open up to you, as well.

This may sound a little arcane, but it's a simple fact of life. What trips people up is that, often, they have no courage for self-revelation, and no vocabulary to describe who they are and what they're looking for in life.

Practicing "courageous conversation" is one way to go about getting these. Developing the habit of authentic dialogue with others can go a long way toward letting them see who you really are and what you need for emotional satisfaction.

Fully Unpacking Postcard Exercise

How open are you? You can use the following postcard exercise to help you review your willingness to unpack your bags with others.

- Who knows you deeply and understands who you really are?

- What would you be unwilling to share with that person? What kinds of things have you been unwilling to share with anyone?

- On the postcard, draw an image or write the name of the person who really knows who you are, who truly sees you.

- Think of the different ways this person allows you to "unpack." List them next to their name or picture. You might even describe an interaction with this person that was particularly fulfilling. Jot down a "thank you for listening" note.

- Send the postcard to them. Wait a few days and then get in touch to do some mutual "unpacking."

CHAPTER 5

Repacking Your Work Bag

How Will I Do My Living?

Since our only possession is our life, or rather our living, our most fundamental question is "How will I do my living?"

The quest for the answer is a lifelong journey. But people don't fully commit to it until they're ready — not one moment sooner. Being ready usually means feeling a level of pain or frustration for which repacking is a remedy.

Readiness emerges at various times during our lives. The common theme is a period of transition. We find ourselves in that in-between state in life, leaving behind an outgrown but still perfectly serviceable past, and moving toward a future that resists all efforts to bring it into clear focus. As we contemplate what's ahead, we feel a strange combination of disorientation and excitement.

Gazing back on our lives is more than just sifting through memories. It also involves poring over images of what the good life has meant to us at various points along the way. We recall the happy times and wonder how many more of them there will be. We review our achievements in life and work and wonder if our best days are behind us — or perhaps, ahead.

Whether consciously or unconsciously, what we often long for most is some way of extricating ourselves from who we've been.

We need some way to break out of the boxes we have built for ourselves. We want to break free, to cast off an old self-image, like a nautilus moving into a new chamber. The same natural process that causes the nautilus to leave old chambers leads human beings to grow new ones.

At times we all wonder if we're alone in our doubts and questioning. And yet we're reticent to share our doubts and questions with others. Most of us, therefore, have what turns out to be a secret longing to discover more in life, to explore "what's next."

Sadly, we end up letting other people take our adventures for us. We let "professional explorers" on the Discovery Channel have the real experience while we participate only vicariously.

But it doesn't have to be this way.

Adventuring, and just as importantly, inventuring — adventuring in the inner world — is possible for all of us, throughout our lives. In fact, if we allow ourselves to, we can make it the focus of our attitudes about life and work.

The big question when we were children was, "what do I want to be when I grow up?" It was too early, perhaps, to ask, "How will I do my living?" The modern dilemma, as sociologist Max Weber put it, is, "Do we work to live, or live to work?"

Many of us will admit that we have lived to work. We've drawn a distinction between what we have to do and what we want to do. But if we're lucky, we can one day discover that the distinction is specious. When we're really adventuring and inventuring, what we have to do merges with what we want to do.

The difficulty, though, is in letting go of all the "have-to's" we've accumulated earlier in life.

Ultimately, what we are searching for is that sense of internal rhythm that explorers feel on their most exciting journeys. It's that feeling of internal and external connectedness: knowing where you're going, but not knowing how to get there. It's about pushing ourselves to new limits, testing our edges, and keeping our curiosity alive.

Living the good life means being a "practical romantic" — seeing the calm beyond the storm and making our way through. We have to deal with making a living, paying college tuitions, loving our partner, doing the right work. We have to pay mortgages and car loans. Thus, we have to continually ask "how will I do my living?" To that extent we have to be practical.

But we also have to be romantic. We have to rekindle our passion. We have to be in love with people, places, and purpose. We have to be willing to engage in the utterly romantic and passionate quest to live the good life. Although we have to be practical and use our heads, we also need to be romantic, and follow our hearts. Even though the path it leads us on wanders all over the place

Life, though, was not meant to be linear. The path from birth to death is not a straight line journey. It's a zig-zag. A loop-the-loop. A switchbacked trail, broken up by much retracing of steps. Our society, however, typically tries to reject this. And the result is the horrifying prospect of ending up "successfully retired," at the end of a linear life.

The linear point of view tells us to first get an education, then work hard, then retire so you can finally begin living. But by that time many people have forgotten how to live — or else they're so exhausted by getting where they've gotten that there's no life left.

The alternative is to live all our life — as fully as possible. To challenge the existing script. To wander as opposed to sticking to the straight and narrow. Of course, this is scary. It's not easy. It means we have to continually ask questions about our life, our love, our work.

On the other hand, there's no escaping it. Sooner or later, in every life, there come times when established patterns, around which we have organized our lives, come apart. We come to question our assumptions about nearly everything. The patterns that have gotten us where we are begin to feel more like heavy weights than reliable guides. We begin the struggle to "let go" — to unpack and repack our bags. We feel like children all over again, and find ourselves asking once more, "What do I want to be when I grow up?"

The truthful answer isn't as simple as it once was. Work has many "truths" for each of us. Since childhood, most of us have thought about what work means, and we constantly scrutinize our assumptions and reframe them as we come of age. Just as love has different meanings at different stages of life, work, too, takes on new meanings along the way.

Here are three "truths" that — at this point in our journey — we think are true about work. It seems to us that these three truths influence, even define, how most people do their living.

Work Truth #1:
People Don't Choose Their Work,
It Chooses Them

Life is not long enough to try everything to discover our right livelihood. Where we grow up, when we grew up, and our vocational family tree all influenced our work choices. How did you choose your work?

Here are some answers we've heard:

- I considered a number of options seriously, explored each one, then picked one. Choosing my work was a difficult decision.

- At an early age I decided what I wanted to do and never considered much else seriously. Choosing my work was easy.

- I didn't have a clue about what I wanted to do; I just took what was available and things developed from there in a way that's kept me satisfied enough.

- I was forced to take whatever job I could find and I just stayed in that field. Through circumstances, my work chose me.

- The decision was more someone else's than mine. It was just expected that I'd enter a certain line of work and I did. I've never committed myself to it, though I'm good at it.

Work satisfaction has a lot to do with how it was chosen. The key ingredient is how consciously and with how much autonomy we've made our choice.

Because most of us don't know who we want to be when we grow up, we must get experience under our belts to be sure of our calling. But by the time we get that experience, some people feel it's too late to make a choice. So they ignore the calling or just refuse to listen. As a result, there are many more people who are never sure of their calling than those who are sure.

During the first part of our lives, someone else usually writes our work script. Later, we are challenged to co-write, edit, or toss the original script.

We are dynamic, not static. We grow and our needs change. False starts or productive mistakes give us a "practice field" to learn what work we most enjoy doing, our calling.

Vocation comes from the Latin *vocare,* to call, and means the work a person is called to from the deepest part of their being.

But the quest for a true calling must be renewed and deepened throughout our lives. Joseph Campbell captured the essence. "The call rings up the curtain, always, on a mystery of transfiguration. The familiar life horizon has been outgrown; the old concepts, ideals and emotional patterns no longer fit; the time for passing the threshold is at hand."

This is often what is happening when we reimagine career changes. We are not just switching jobs; we are pursuing our calling. And this requires crossing a threshold into a deeper part of ourselves.

Work Truth #2:
People Are More Sure of
What They DON'T Love to Do
Than What They DO Love to Do

Ask many people what their talents are and how they enjoy expressing them, and they'll tell you they don't know. But ask them what
they don't like and what they can't do, and you'll get a list a yard long.
Experience has educated them in the negatives, but done little to in-
form them about the positives. This makes sense, actually. In order to
truly dislike something, we have to experience it.

Try this out. Consider what are the two or three worst jobs
you've ever had. What did you like least about them? What kind of
people did you work with? What did you learn about what not to do
in the future?

Hopefully, the jobs that you hated most came earlier in your work
life. When we're first starting out, we often have to take jobs we don't
like — just to make ends meet. We're forced to try a lot of jobs that
we wouldn't otherwise think of.

For most of us, when we're younger, the problem isn't just that
we don't know what we like — we also don't know what we're good
at. We haven't identified our talents. Or even if we have, we haven't
developed confidence in them. Or in ourselves. Belief in yourself
comes from the knowledge that you have the talents to be what you
want to be.

Talents are a source of energy within each of us that is always
waiting to be discovered (or rediscovered) and expressed. Tarthong
Tulku, a lama from Eastern Tibet, speaks of this in his book *Skillful
Means*. "By using skillful means to enrich our lives and bring our creature potential into everything we do, we can penetrate to the heart of
our true nature. We then gain an understanding of the basic purpose

in life, and appreciate the job of making good use of our precious time and energy."

This knowledge of what we call doing the right work, together with a strong sense of talents and purpose in life, is an essential part of answering the question, "How will I do my living?"

In their classic *Living the Good Life*, Helen and Scott Nearing propose that the "objective of economic effort is not money, but livelihood." They explain that the purpose of working is not to "make money" or "get rich," but rather, to secure an existence that is harmonious with one's deepest beliefs and most powerful feelings. In 1954, when their book was first published, they noted they knew of few people who shared their attitude, and that this was the source of much of the hardship — economic as well as emotional — that they observed. No doubt the numbers are no greater today . . . and the hardship certainly no less.

A high percentage of people who truly feel that they are living the good life have work that uses their best-loved talents as opposed to a job they do mainly to earn money.

Walter Kerr, in *The Decline of Pleasure,* writes, "If I were required to put it into a single sentence, my own explanation of the state of our hearts, heads and nerves, I would do it this way: we are vaguely wretched because we are leading half-lives, half-hearted, and with only one-half of our minds actively engaged in making contact with the universe about us."[10]

To say that many people feel half-alive at work is probably an understatement. In our interviews, a much more common complaint is that they feel "half-dead." People are secretly frantic. They sleepwalk through their days, half-heartedly using half their minds, but at the same time, they're terrified that they're wasting potentially half of their one and only life.

Each of us wants to feel unique. And what most of us mean by that is that we hope to discover some innate specialness which is our birthright, which no one else has in quite the same way. Ironically, most of us are so scared to be different that we hide our uniqueness any time it rears its ugly head.

So, we're hungry to discover and express our talents because we need to be reassured of our uniqueness. We all want to feel that we're not just another grain of sand on the beach but that we've been put here for some unique purpose — a purpose no one else can fulfill.

When it comes to acknowledging or owning our talents, most of us are terminally blind. We're taught not to brag or extol our virtues. Richard Bach notes in his book, *Illusions*, "Argue for your limitations and sure enough they're yours!"[11]

Everyone has some excellence seeking expression. Everyone has talents of which they are unaware or which they downplay. Uncovering those talents involves a learning process which has steps to it, much like the process by which one learns to ride a bike or to swim. Each step has to be mastered before the next step can be approached. But like riding a bike, once you've got it mastered, you never forget!

Work Truth #3:
Work Repacking Is a Critical Survival Skill Today

The idea of a permanent job is obsolete. These days, no one's job is safe! The work world is in constant turmoil. Once-powerful industries teeter on the brink of extinction. Companies whose names used to be synonymous with security are laying people off in record numbers. Your job may disappear at any moment without warning. These days, nearly everyone will be "between jobs" or out of work at some time.

It doesn't even matter how good a job you're doing. Excellence is no defense. You solve problems creatively? You consistently add value? These are no longer safeguards against searing competition, rapid technological change, and relentless restructuring.

You must be prepared to go job-hunting for the rest of your life. No one owes you a job — not your present employer, not your union, not even if you work for Mom and Dad. It's up to you to create your future. Today, everyone, up through the highest ranks of professionals, feel increased pressure to reinvent themselves as a marketable "portfolio" of talents.

As the paradigm of work shifts to a "creator economy," work itself is being redefined. We're seeing an increased need for re-learning and creative thinking, less focus on "what you know" than "how you add value."

All of us will be unpacking and repacking the structure of our work. Most of us will end up working for a "network" of organizations linked to customers and suppliers via technology. If you've been keeping up with your reading, you'll recognize this model as the "networked society" — a place pared down to its core competencies and sending out for everything else — including lunch!

In the future, the key question for most people will not be "What's my job?" — but "What value do I add?"

So it's time to ask yourself that same question.

What value do I add?

Too many of us define ourselves these days by our "tools." When someone asks us what we do, we say, "Oh, I work with computers." Or, "I'm in technology." Even highly trained professionals define themselves like this: "I'm a radiologist." Or "I run a network."

The problem is that many, if not most, of those tools are going to be obsolete in a few years. So if you've built a career based on your tools, you'll be out of luck. And out of work, too.

Instead of getting known for your tools, you need to build a reputation based on the distinct value you can offer.

Regardless of where you work these days — at a large corporation, a small business, or at a computer in your basement — the message is the same. You are on your own. You have to see yourself as a business. You have to consider yourself your own corporation, "You, Inc.," and like any corporation, be ready to develop a comprehensive strategic plan for growth.

If we can recycle bottles, cans, and newspapers, we can certainly "recycle" ourselves. To prosper in this volatile world of work we must be ready to recycle ourselves. In other words, to repack our bags.

And even if this weren't the case, even if the workaday world was as stable and predictable as in years gone by, there's an even more important reason why life and work repacking is a critical survival skill:

Most of us tire of our work once we have mastered it.

Feeling burnt-out? Rusted-out? Bored? Maybe you've reached the end of the road on your current job.

All jobs have "lives": cycles of learning, mastery, plateauing, and declining.

Because we have brains, we require new stimulation for growth, food for the mind, body, and soul. Some people try to ignore this. Others create life crises on purpose. A friend of ours claims, "Three years is enough for anyone in one job path. After that it's a repeat performance. The fun challenges will have been met and creativity expressed. Your curiosity fades, productivity flattens and numbness settles in!"

When Hall of Fame baseball player George Brett ended his career after 20 record-breaking seasons, he admitted that his desire had waned. He said, "I wasn't that excited when I did something good. I wasn't getting that down when I did something bad. I wasn't that happy when we won. I didn't feel as bad when we lost. There's something about riding a roller coaster. If you ride a roller coaster 162 times, you're ready for something different."

The Ideal Job?

Many people have settled for work that makes them mildly miserable day after day, month after month, year after year. When they feel the pangs of frustration or burnout, they attempt to bury their fear. They rationalize, "Hey, it's a living! What more can you ask for these days?"

The message is that drudgery is tolerable as long as it pays.

Our response to these people is probably exactly what they don't want to hear. First, we believe that all the money in the world doesn't make drudgery tolerable. And second, we're convinced that you don't have to settle for less than your dreams. It is possible to find the job you really want. Such good fortune is not just for a lucky few.

Everyone knows what the "ideal job" is: you get paid a huge sum of money to work in a lovely office all by yourself with unlimited travel to beautiful places and lots of time off. And nobody tells you what to do.

But the truth is, that ideal job doesn't exist. Not if you define it the way most people do — as one that has no bad parts to it, no "latrine work."

Every job has its good parts and its bad parts. It's hard to imagine any kind of work that would be enjoyable 100% of the time. Even sports heroes and movie stars have their bad days.

So, the "ideal job" isn't really about full-time enjoyment. Instead, it's one that mirrors perfectly the person who holds it. And people do find — or invent, or create — these jobs. They do it by working a process — a surprisingly simple one.

It's a process that links who you are with what you do.

The process involves developing a clarity about your talents, passions, and values: looking inside yourself to discover what you love to do, what you truly care about, and the type of working environment that supports what you care about most. And then combining all three to develop a clear vision of the kind of work that links who you are with what you do.

When we talk with those who are energized by their work, who are truly enjoying it, we notice they are not in "perfect jobs." But, they are in situations that they have freely chosen. If and when they change work directions or retire, they eventually "choose" something again.

Many do a combination of things as they reach for a quality of life that involves, as Robert Fulghum writes in *All I Really Need To Know I Learned In Kindergarten,* "learning some and thinking some and drawing and painting and singing and dancing and playing and working every day some."

The ideal job isn't a standard of living — it's a state of mind and a state of being. In the ideal job, you're applying the talents you enjoy most to an interest you're passionate about, in an environment that fits who you are and what you value.

The Reimagined Life

We're inspired by stories of people whose talents, passions, and values are in alignment, and who have the courage and conviction to regularly reimagine and recreate their work lives. We've noticed common threads running through their stories, and have taken to calling this the "reimagined life."

Here are some of the common threads of people who are living the reimagined life:

- They have a purpose larger than their own needs, wants and desires — a sense of how their lives and work fit into the larger scheme of things.

- They have an internal compass which keeps them "truing" to their purpose in life.

- They have clear boundaries around their two most precious currencies — time and money.
- They have a sense of their potential talents, the limits of which have not been fully tested.
- They have marked adaptability when faced with obstacles — they simply handle them as a natural feature of living.
- Their abundant energy is infectious — it gives them and the people around them even more.
- They see their work as more than just a job; they are motivated by a sense of "calling."
- They have a feeling of lightness — a sense of not being burdened by the burdens they are carrying.

We often hear about "visionaries": inspiring people whose lives center around their talents, passions, and values. People, who, to paraphrase George Bernard Shaw, "dream of things that never were and ask, 'Why not?'"

Understandably, we tend to put such people on a pedestal, and convince ourselves that we could never be like them; that they have something we could never have.

It's true, most of them do have something few of us have, but it's false that it's unavailable to us. In fact, the main difference that we've observed between these "visionaries" and the rest of us can be observed in just two simple qualities:

First, these "visionaries" tend to have clearly identified for themselves their *purpose* — their source of meaning in life, the reason they "get up in the morning."

And second, they view work as a *calling,* a vocation, as something they were meant to do. In short, they have discovered work that is rich in purpose.

Choosing Work That Is Rich in Purpose

What is the purpose of your work?

Before choosing work that is rich in purpose, we must first clarify what our work's purpose is. To put it another way, if we don't know what we want, how will we know if we've gotten it?

But even before knowing *what* we want, we need to know *why* we want it. Knowing why we want something means knowing a little bit more about our purpose in life.

So what is "purpose"?

Purpose is your reason for being, your answer to the question, "Why do I get up in the morning?" It is the spiritual core that helps us find the aliveness in our day-to-day work life. Nevertheless, for a lot of us, the "purpose" aspect of our lives is the hardest to understand because it can't really be measured and it's hard to see.

A purpose is not a goal. A goal is something that can be reached. A purpose, though, is never achieved. It exists before you, and lives on after you're gone.

Purpose is a direction, like "west." No matter how far west you go, there's still more west to travel. And like directions, a purpose helps you choose where to go along the route.

Purpose is your lodestar, your personal compass of truth. It tells you, in any given moment, whether you're living your life "on purpose" or not.

You use your purpose to set your course in life. It's the quality around which you center yourself. Without a clear sense of purpose it's like being on a ship without a rudder somewhere in the middle of an ocean — you're lost, and out of control. Having a purpose, though, enables you to find your direction. It makes choosing the right work enormously easier.

Often it takes a crisis for people to discover (or rediscover) their calling — their authentic work. Here are some questions, though, that can lead you to uncover your calling.

1. What are your talents?
    Name all of them — this is no time for modesty. Then choose three you think are most important and write them down. Narrow down each to one or two words. "Loving, caring, teaching, listening, creating, etc." If you're blocked, ask a Repacking Partner for suggestions.

    > *Richard's example:* "My three most important talents are my deep listening ability, my simplifying, and clear speaking."

    > *Dave's example:* "My three most important talents are my sense of humor, my optimism, and my resourcefulness."

2. What are you passionate about?
    What are the things you are most curious about, that you daydream about, that you wish you had more time to put energy into? What needs doing in the world that you'd like to put your talents to work on? What are the main areas in which you'd like to invest your talents?

    > *Richard's example:* "My passion or focus is to help people awaken their spirit for the sake of discovering their purpose in life."

    > *Dave's example:* "My passion is on helping people to communicate more effectively, and in doing so, to foster understanding among individuals and communities."

3. What environment feels most natural to you?
    In what work and life situations are you most comfortable expressing your talents?

    > *Richard's example:* "I most often express my talents and interest in casual learning settings (e.g., workshops) or sitting around campfires with people."

> *Dave's example: "I most often express my talents in a one-on-one situation, either with another person or with myself."*

4. Now take your answers to questions 1, 2 and 3, and combine what you think are the most important elements of them to make a complete sentence as in the following example from Richard:

> *"My purpose in life is . . . " (answer to question 1): "to use my listening, my simplifying and my clear speaking"*
>
> *(answer to question 2): "to help people awaken their spirits"*
>
> *(answer to question 3): "in natural environments."*
>
> *Richard says, "Over the years my purpose has evolved to one simple statement that moves me: "To help people awaken their spirits."*

It's important that you state your purpose in the present tense to ensure that it is always current. Again, you'll probably find that, in many ways, you've already been living your purpose all along. The choices you have made throughout your life have supported it. It does help, though, particularly during work changes, to have your purpose statement clearly in mind. That way the stresses make more sense and you're better able to connect the changes to new insights and healthy choices.

One last note: You may find you have several purposes — several issues you care deeply about. If you keep investigating, though, you'll eventually find a common thread that ties them all together. So, repeat the questions above as often as you wish to clarify your moving purpose.

Identifying Your Calling

Calling is the inner urge to give our gifts away. We heed that call when we offer our gifts in service to something we are passionate about in an environment that is consistent with our core values.

The roots of calling in our lives go back very deeply — to even before we were born. Calling is an expression of our essence; it's our embedded destiny. The seed of this destiny lies within us; one way or another it seeks to fulfill itself in the world. So the question we need to ask ourselves is whether we're doing all we can to bring the fruits of our calling to bear.

Although calling runs through our whole lives, we are not called once for life. It is something we do every day. Calling breaks down into daily choices. Responding to our calling, we ask ourselves again and again: "How can I consistently give my gifts away?"

We bring our calling to our work every single day. And we do so by expressing our gifts, passions, and values in a manner that is consistent with the legacy we want to leave.

People who have discovered their calling and choose to bring it to their work tend to be phenomenally energized about what they do. They have an almost childlike passion for their projects and a great sense of gratitude for their good fortune. By aligning who they are with what they do, they have answered the eternal question we face every day: "Why do I get up in the morning?"

Discovering that calling, though, can be made easier through the use of the Calling Cards — a list of natural preferences that have emerged in our discussions and research with hundreds of people over the last few decades. Each of the callings describes a core gift. Each calling comes directly out of someone's experience. We have been collecting callings in seminars, workshops, and coaching sessions with individuals and groups from all walks of life. The list of 52 callings we have come up with represent the "essence of essences" in our research. (This doesn't mean that there are not other callings than our 52; it does, however, mean that these 52 represent those that have best withstood real-world testing.)

Using the Calling Cards in a simple self-examination helps us name our calling — that gift which is invisible but wants to be un-wrapped and given away.

The lives we live emerge from the words we choose to define our lives. So, as you examine the Calling Cards, listen carefully to what you're telling yourself. To find joy in our work, we need a clear, simple way to name our calling. We need to reframe our concept of calling until the words feel natural and come to us easily. We must settle for nothing less than a description of calling that fits us and no one else exactly the same way. No one can choose our calling for us; no one else can tell us how to express our calling once it is found. Each of us, individually, must hear and heed our role in the world. Each of us must choose or create the Calling Card that expresses the gifts we feel an inner urge to give away.

So . . . go within. Examine the Calling Cards. Explore the pos-sibilities of calling. Name your calling.

Calling Cards Instructions

Step 1: Your Natural Preferences

Ask yourself: What do I love to do?

Examine the entire list of 52 callings. As you study them, ar-range the callings in three groups according to your natural pref-erences.

Group #1: Those that fit what you truly love to do.

Group #2: Those that are not things you love to do.

Group #3: Not sure or can't decide right now.

Don't rush. Use your intuition. What does your hand turn to naturally? What calls to you? Continue to look through the first two groups to identify those callings that fit you best.

(An interactive online version of the Calling Cards is available at www.inventuregroup.com.)

List of Calling Cards

CONVENTIONAL
Organizing Things
Getting Things Right
Operating Things
Processing Things
Doing the Numbers
Straightening Things Up

REALISTIC
Building Things
Fixing Things
Making Things Work
Shaping Environments
Growing Things
Solving Problems
Moving Physically

INVESTIGATIVE
Advancing Ideas
Discovering Resources
Researching Things
Getting to the Heart of Matters
Investigating Things
Making Connections
Putting the Pieces Together
Translating Things
Analyzing Information

ENTERPRISING
Persuading People
Exploring the Way
Opening Doors
Bringing Out Potential
Selling Intangibles
Managing Things
Empowering Others
Starting Things
Making Deals

SOCIAL
Awakening Spirit
Bringing Joy
Creating Trust
Facilitating Change
Creating Dialogue
Helping Overcome Obstacles
Building Relationships
Giving Care
Instructing People
Resolving Disputes
Getting Participation
Healing Wounds

ARTISTIC
Adding Humor
Breaking Molds
Designing Things
Seeing Possibilities
Composing Themes
Seeing the Big Picture
Writing Things
Creating Things
Performing Events

Step 2: Your Five Most Natural Preferences

> *Ask yourself: What five gifts do I most love to do?*

Concentrate on the Group #1 callings. Explore them more carefully. Which ones seem to be the "best of the best"? Without thinking too much about it, identify the ones that seem to call to you automatically. Select the top five callings from this group — those that best describe what you naturally enjoy doing.

Step 3: Your Single Most Natural Preference

> *Ask yourself: What gift do I most love to give to others?*

Consider the five callings you have selected. Knowing yourself as you do, which one card seems to "call to you"; which is the one that, throughout your life, you have most consistently loved giving to others? If you were forced to pick just one, which one would it be?

Step 4: Your Calling Card

Study your number one card. If the words don't fit exactly, feel free to edit so that your own calling describes you accurately. You may find it useful to use words from your top five callings to perfectly describe your calling.

Step 5: Make a Call

Discuss your Calling Card with a Repacking Partner. See if others have insight into your calling that can help you refine it further.

Step 6: Imagine a Call

Imagine that you could do any kind of work in the world; anything at all — *as long as it fits your Calling Card.* Jot down three or four things you can see yourself doing. What does this list tell you about your calling?

Step 7: Heed the Call

>   Perhaps you're thinking: "This Calling Card looks great. But
>   it's not my job! Moreover, I don't have the financial resources
>   or personal freedom to do the work I love the most. How do I
>   heed the call when I first have to heed my bills, my boss, and my
>   family?" If you're asking questions like that, ask yourself these
>   questions instead:

- Does your work give you a small opportunity to express your
  calling? Does it ever let you do what you most enjoy doing?

- While you're working, do you ever get the sense that you're doing the right thing in the right place? How often does it happen?
  When it happens, what are you doing?

- What's one thing — a little thing — you could do right now to
  express your calling at work? What's stopping you?

Another Way to Use the Calling Cards

An alternative way to arrive at Your Single Most Natural Preference is
to work through the callings, pairing them two-by-two, and choosing
which of the pair you think more accurately reflects your calling. This
works especially well with a partner.

Set the callings down between you and your partner. Have your
partner name the first two callings. Quickly — within three seconds
or so — choose which is the better expression of what you most love
to do. Put the "winner" in one group, and set the "loser" aside. (If you
honestly can't decide — that is, if they're both "winners," put them
both in the "winning" group. If neither seems appropriate for you at
all, discard them both.)

Having gone through the callings once, you will have a group of
26 winners. Repeat the process from above, going through all 26.
Now you will have 13 winners. Repeat the process with this group.

You'll have six winners. Then three. Then one. This final "winning" card is your Calling Card.

Get Into It!

Having chosen our Calling Card, we are faced with the unavoidable choice of whether to heed it. Either we do or we don't — and the time to decide has arrived.

Calling isn't our work, it's what we *bring to* our work. The core idea of calling is a simple and liberating truth: "It's not what you do that matters, it's how you do it."

In order to understand this aspect of calling more fully, it's helpful to ask yourself two questions. The first is *"What do you do?"* What kind of work are you currently performing? How consistent is it with your stated calling? Should you stay or leave your current job? The second question is *"How do you do it?"* What part of your job fulfills your sense of calling? How can you give away your gifts, even if you're in a job that isn't exactly what you want to be doing? How can you express your calling, even if only partially?

Elements of our calling can be expressed in almost any job. When we begin to see what we do as an opportunity for heeding our calling, nothing changes — but everything changes. We still have our reports to write, our students to teach, our clients to serve. We still have our up days and down days; empowering colleagues and irritating colleagues; interesting projects and boring projects. We still have days when it's hard to get out of bed in the morning. Nothing seems to have changed.

But on the other hand, everything has changed. By expressing our calling, even in small, partial ways, our work is suddenly more fulfilling. We find meaning in what we do, even when it's not exactly what we think we were meant to be doing. On occasion, throughout the work day, we feel that we're in the right place, with the right people, doing the right work, on purpose.

We have, in other words, found that formula for reimagining our lifework.

"Get a Life"

With a clearly identified calling in our lives, we are ready and able to reimagine our lifework. We are finally able to lighten up and live — quite simply, to "get a life."

The word "light" in the word "enlightened" is often thought of in the sense of illumination. Enlightened people have "seen the light" or "see things in a new light." There is, however, another use of the word "enlighten" — that is, "a lightening of the load."

In *The White Hole In Time,* Peter Russell explains, "The heaviest burdens in this life are not our physical burdens but our mental ones. We are weighed down by our concern for the past and our worries about the future. This is the load we bear, the weariness that comes from our timefulness . . . To enlighten the mind is to relieve it of this load. An enlightened mind is a mind no longer weighed down by attachments; it is a mind that is free."[12]

Dante was 35 years old and frustrated with his life when he wrote the first line of *The Inferno* — describing perhaps the first midlife crisis in Western literature.

Midway through life's journey I was made aware that I had strayed into a dark forest, and the right path appeared not anywhere.

However it is described, middle age remains a key period in people's lives in which they choose to lighten their loads.

Many people ask themselves, "Wasn't I supposed to be somebody by now, or at least to know what I want to do with my life?"

Our investigations lead us to conclude that there are no set stages, transition points or predictable crises. What happens to people is often the result of accident, personal experiences, financial circumstances, and the historical period in which they live. People naturally move in and out of phases of life.

What does commonly happen, however, is a more subtle acceptance of life's limitations and possibilities. One of two things seems to happen by midlife: we achieve our dream or we do not. Either way it creates a problem. The sooner we accept the idea that life may not turn out as we originally planned, the more likely we are to reimagine our lives in a positive manner. Often a major life event — divorce, illness, losing a job, kids leaving home (or returning), or the deaths of parents, spouses and friends — can bring about profound reimagining. These can happen at any point in life, but they seem to mount up in midlife and beyond. Our ability to prepare for and respond to these challenges is what reimagining our lives is all about.

Life Reimagined Postcard Exercise

Try to imagine how your life reimagined could look. Here's an opportunity to clarify your vision.

Directions

- On your postcard, write down your Life Reimagined Formula: (Talents $\times$ Passions $\times$ Environment) $=$ Calling

- Imagine that you are living that life. Write a couple of sentences describing the work that you'd love to do. It need not be an essay, but make it more than "Weather's fine, wish you were here."

- Send your postcard to your Repacking Partner. If possible, get together with them to converse about your Life Reimagined.

CHAPTER 6

Repacking On Purpose

How Much Is Enough?

At many points on our journey through life, we have to decide what to take along and what to leave behind — and once we decide, how to carry it.

Carrying too much weighs us down so heavily with work, people, and possessions that we are exhausted before we reach our destination. Carrying too little leaves us isolated and vulnerable, with little chance of reaching our goals. Our only hope of success is to first take stock of what we need and then, figure out what's the best way to carry the load.

So we need to ask ourselves a couple of questions. First, in general, "How much is enough?" And second, in relation to each specific item, "What do I really want to carry?"

We also have to recognize that no matter how well we plan, our needs will change along the way. Many of the things we lay out on the bed before the trip come to seem a lot less important once we're on the road. It's through experience that we figure out what's really essential and how much we can comfortably carry. As a result, we often need to lighten our load along the way — not just physically, but psychologically, as well. Every step up the mountain, we must ask ourselves "What do we really need?"

The late John Williamson was a Harvard-educated, articulate spokesman for lifelong learning and new educational technologies. As a senior executive with Wilson Learning Corporation he mingled with the leading thinkers on change and leadership.

Richard remembers John like this:

> I knew him as a friend, a colleague, and in his last eighteen months as a client, as he fought valiantly against his cancer while simultaneously envisioning his future. During that time, I often flashed back to scenes of him backpacking and interacting with the Maasai in Africa, so curious, so alive.
>
> Just one day away from the end of his life, he talked about his impending losses. I sat by his bed, holding his hand. He laughed and wept unashamedly as he talked about our work together.
>
> Staring out the window, struggling to see with his one remaining good eye, he said to me, "I always thought God had a plan for me to do something special in this life, but I never really found out what it was. I feel as if I never really found out who I wanted to be when I grew up."
>
> That statement penetrated my core. We wept together as he encouraged my work. "Push them to make a difference," he said, "and don't let them off the hook."
>
> He died the next day.

John's words are a reminder to us that beyond all else is the driving need for each of us to "make a difference"; to believe that our lives have counted.

By finding our purpose — whatever it is — we make our contribution, however large or small, to our time. We discover, and bring to life for ourselves, what John called "God's plan." Discovering this plan, reimagining it as needed, is a lifelong project. One step that can assist in this, though, is a simple taking stock — what we call the Repacking Inventory.

Repacking Inventory

You do this every day. An inventory is simply asking yourself "What do I have?" Rushing around the house searching for your car keys is one kind of inventory. Tearing through your closet looking for one last blouse or clean shirt to wear is another. The Repacking Inventory takes that natural activity one step further, to a process that is slightly more structured.

No matter what form it takes, inventorying is an activity from which we all can learn something. When was the last time you moved? As you packed box after box after box, were you amazed by how much stuff you'd accumulated over the period you'd lived in your house? Did you wish you'd taken the opportunity to do some sorting and winnowing out beforehand?

Dave remembers how his inventory has grown:

> The first time I made a major move in my life (from Pittsburgh to San Francisco after high school), I fit everything I owned into one very large knapsack. Five years later, moving to Los Angeles, I carried three suitcases on the airplane. Four years after that, when I moved to Santa Fe, New Mexico, my possessions filled up the entire back seat of my Chevy Nova. In Santa Fe, I got married, and when my wife, Jennifer, and I moved to Minnesota a few years later, we required a 12-foot panel truck. The last time we moved, which was after five years in Seattle, it took a full-sized moving van and three large young men to transport our worldly goods.

Not all of this accumulation is mindless. But not all is mindful either. The point of your inventory is to simply check out what's there.

So we encourage you now to do a quick inventory of your stuff. Take fifteen or twenty minutes to mentally or physically wander through your life. Consider all the things you're carrying. Open all your closets. How much of your accumulation is mindful? And how much is just stuff that's piled up?

In other words, how much is helping you get where you're going and how much is just weighing you down?

Imagine Aging

There are many ways for people of even modest means to escape the trap of carrying too much, or too much of the wrong thing. All involve making decisions about what really matters.

It is possible for harried people to live much as they do now and be much happier. It all boils down to where you end up on two questions:

- "How much is enough?"
- "What do I really want to carry?"

In answering these questions, many people make the choice to live a "life reimagined." Indeed, many find that coming to grips with those two questions is the key to improving their quality of life.

Answering these two questions is an important step towards bringing your own lifestyle and workstyle into balance. It can also be a ticket to personal fulfillment — to a life that is simpler, less cluttered, yet rich with purpose and meaning.

This is the sort of life that more and more people are aspiring to, especially those who are facing the inevitable life transitions that come with age. So it's not surprising that the organization AARP (formerly known as the American Association of Retired Persons) has embarked on a new journey to help its members do just that — to "reimagine" their lives.

AARP started the project by confronting a five-letter word that seemed to make everyone who heard it slightly uncomfortable. That word: "aging."

What AARP found odd was that while most people in their membership demographic seem to embrace (rather than fear) getting older, they don't like to talk about aging — probably because they don't even think of themselves as old. Many see themselves as in better shape — intellectually, emotionally, even physically — than they were when they were younger. Consequently, their talk tends to avoid references to time and stage of life. They're okay with aging as it's happening to them; they just don't see themselves as candidates for an organization defined by aging. To do so would denote a pessimism about the years ahead that most reject. By contrast, they see what's to come as potentially better and better.

Why does this group exhibit such optimism about the future, especially during current times of intense economic and social stress? For one thing, they've embraced the notion of "repacking." They don't see themselves cornered into the same life structure as their parents, and they're not going to seek permission to repack if they want to shift gears. On the contrary, they see repacking as a natural and essential part of life.

They're living longer and healthier lives. They're doing and contributing more, in longer working lives. In a world filled with more of everything, more years means more time to do and be more things. From the outside, it might look like they're trying to reject getting older; from the inside, though, it's simply about redefining what "getting older" means. It turn outs that wanting to feel young and alive, while at the same time not being afraid of aging, go hand in hand.

This is where AARP's "life reimagined project" comes in. It asks us to imagine new ways to easily and instantaneously connect with others who similarly engaged in the repacking process. Imagine having a question, a fear, a dream, or a goal, and being able to connect with just the right person to assist us on our journey of discovery. Imagine physical and virtual spaces that enable us to more successfully navigate emerging life challenges in the new "creator economy." Imagine resources that help us live our best life at every new stage — to continually support us in addressing the "what's next?" questions as they arise.

It used to be that repacking was essentially a midlife endeavor, a mid-course correction to set us on our way for the second half of life. That model itself has now been repacked. As AARP's project now highlights, repacking unfolds continually, at each moment as we reimagine our lives.

Richard recently passed a man sweeping the sidewalks on 53rd Street in New York City. He wore the uniform of city maintenance workers but sported a T-shirt that read, on the front, "Imagine," and on the back, "No matter what you're doing."

It made Richard wonder: what if we invested every action we take with imagination? What if sweeping sidewalks, cooking meals, even writing a report for work or school were filled with conscious imagining and reimagining?

Repacking: The "What Is a Life Reimagined?" Question

We've come now to the part where it's all supposed to happen — Repacking Your Bags . . . this is it!

So now what?

Maybe you feel like you're in the opening scene in the classic film, *The Graduate,* where Dustin Hoffman, as Benjamin, the newly minted college graduate, having finally arrived at where he's been heading all his young life, has no idea where he wants to go. His father's business partner exhorts him to get into "plastics," but this provides no comfort or direction. The only place Benjamin feels at all consoled is at the bottom of his family's swimming pool, safely secluded in scuba gear and goggles.

Maybe it's like that.

Unfortunately, we can't offer you a one word answer like "plastics" to the question "Now what?"

We can, however, remind you that you've done this many times before. Although now you may have a better understanding than ever before of what repacking involves, you should recall that this isn't the first time you've done it.

Any time you've ever moved, gone to a new school, started a different job, fallen in love with another person, even taken a vacation, you've repacked on some level. You've considered the things that matter most to you, thought about how they fit into the life ahead of you, and made decisions accordingly. You've made choices, set some things aside, learned new skills for the journey ahead, and set off.

You've unpacked and repacked, and since you're here, still in one piece, and reading this, you've obviously done so with some success — even if it's not at the level you'd like. Earlier in this book, even, you've used tools like The Good Life Checklist (page 185) to help set up for repacking.

All this has helped prepare the ground for the process at hand. The difference is that now you've got a framework for your repacking. A model for where things go and — we hope, anyway — a better idea of how to go about arranging them. You might think of it like the interior of padded cases for carrying electronic equipment. With any luck, repacking now feels more like you're arranging each item in its own well-designed cutout, whereas before, you were just jumbling everything up in a formless duffel.

Lots of times what really stops people from doing this is the fear of committing to something new. It's the feeling that the decision is just too big to make. We feel that we must decide "now" how we're going to spend "the rest of our lives!" We see the life/work decisions as being too important — so crucial and overwhelming that we can't bear to face them. So we avoid repacking until the last possible moment. Or until it's too late.

Too often when we're faced with decisions like this, their importance paralyzes us. The weight of future possibilities crushes us and we end up entirely unable to make a decision at all.

But you can overcome your own fear by keeping in mind that the decisions you make aren't cast in concrete. Remember, repacking is a cradle-to-grave process. It's more than likely that one day in the not-too-distant future, you'll be repacking whatever repacking you do now.

It's Not Earth Shoes

As you get into the process of repacking, you may begin to feel some trepidation about what in the world you've gotten yourself into. Maybe the life you've "always wanted" *isn't* actually the life you really want. Maybe things are fine the way they are. Maybe you're not ready for a change.

Well, relax. No matter what you decide, what conclusions you come to, or what decisions you make, "it's not Earth Shoes."

Not Earth Shoes?

Back in the 1970s a friend of ours, Chad Worcester, bought a pair of "Earth Shoes." If you were born after 1965 or so, you probably don't remember them; if you were born before then, you'd probably prefer to forget them. In any case, they were soft-sided shoes that featured a recessed heel, which supposedly enabled you to walk more naturally than in regular shoes. They were probably just as well-known for their advertising — a footprint in the sand, showing how naturally our heels sink down when we walk.

Earth Shoes weren't the most attractive shoes ever made, but they did have their fifteen minutes of fame. Chad bought himself a pair and walked out onto the sidewalk wearing them. He looked down at his feet and thought how strange his shoes looked. He strolled around a bit and felt how strange they felt. It struck him that their shape and feel would take some real getting used to.

Turning around, he saw a sign in the shoe store advertising Earth Shoes. It read, "Earth Shoes. The last pair of shoes you'll ever own."

Chad found the idea that this was "it," and that Earth Shoes were that "it," too much to take. He wasn't ready for the last pair of shoes he'd ever own. So he turned right around and traded his Earth Shoes in for a pair of sneakers.

So, keep in mind that however you repack, it's not the last opportunity you'll ever have to do so. Whatever decision you make, remember, it's not Earth Shoes.

What You Don't Have to Do

We'll also remind you that repacking isn't some mysterious process for which you have no prior experience. Don't forget: you've done this all before.

Repacking may be like exercise, but it isn't the loneliness of the long-distance runner. That's why we encourage you to repack with a Repacking Partner, or check in regularly as you do so. Putting the process into words with another person allows you to test your theories and ideas before you put them into practice. You're less likely to go off the deep end (not always a mistake, but not always the right thing to do, either) if you talk things over with someone else first.

In order to repack, you DON'T have to:

• Do it all by yourself without help or support from anyone.

• Climb to a mountaintop and commune with the One-ness of everything.

- Sell all your worldly possessions and start over from scratch.

- Quit your job.

- Join the Peace Corps.

- Move from where you're living.

- Get a divorce or get married.

- Solve all the world's problems. (Or even all of your own.)

- Finish the entire process in a single sitting.

- Be afraid to change any conclusions at which you arrive.

- Be afraid to change, period.

Midlife Repackings

Our culture's conception of age is out of touch with today's reality. In jest, people say that "50 is the new 40," but, in fact, most adults at age 50 have more years ahead of them than earlier generations did at age 30 or so. Life expectancy in the West is at 80-plus and rising. This means that at midlife, many will live another four decades or so. The average baby boomer, at "retirement age," has as many years of creative living ahead of her as she has behind.

As more of us live — and stay healthier — longer, more of us will find repacking to be an existential necessity. Some of this repacking will be inner-driven; dissatisfaction or a desire for something new will be the impetus. Other midlife revisions will be inspired by external events: job losses, the deaths of loved ones, health challenges. But whatever the cause, some form of midlife reinvention is inevitable.

Nevertheless, in spite of the frequency and obvious necessity of such change, midlife remains a mysterious and confusing period, and one for which most of us are, on the whole, ill-prepared. No surprise that it's also a time when many people feel especially inadequate.

The good news, however, is that years and dozens of university-based studies on the over-50 age group reveal clearly that midlife can be a uniquely energizing time. Most people, by this stage in their lives, have developed a clearer sense of who they really are. And typically — though not always — they are in a better position than ever before to reflect upon their lives and challenge even their most basic assumptions about it. Consequently the potential for profound and meaningful change is quite high.

The last few decades have seen a rapid increase in the number of people who identify themselves as "spiritual but not religious." This is a hopeful sign, because it means that without a belief in something greater than themselves more and more people are searching for something that is missing in their lives, something that exists both within and without. It's an indication of a shared recognition that much of what preoccupies us doesn't really matter in the long run.

We live in a society that gives us instant access via computers and mobile phones to a virtual version of each other, but leaves us longing for authentic human connection. Something more, something greater needs to pass between us, and that's what people are searching for when they seek their own spirituality.

For this more meaningful connection to occur, we need to pay a higher quality of attention to one another. This isn't the same as simply paying "more" attention to each other. What connects people is compassion, a depth that happens when we genuinely listen. The value of genuinely listening to each other, regardless of whether we agree on things, seems to be almost completely lost in an age of busyness and hurry sickness. The challenge is to create genuine presence, the kind of authentic being-with-each-other that may actually bring about real relationships and support positive change.

Midlife repacking requires us to transform two fundamental life practices: the *relational* practices, or how we interact with other people and living things, and the *creative* practices, or how we manifest meaning in our daily lives. Interwoven, these two strands form the thread of our lives in renewal.

The thread reminds us that we can't expect to renew ourselves in a piecemeal fashion. Because the thread holds everything together, change in one aspect of our lives necessarily affects the others. We grow as whole persons or not at all. Without the thread, we remain half-children, living half-lives.

The larger fabric woven by the thread is the strengthening of connections, connections that are fundamental to midlife health, healing, happiness, and holiness. Holding on to the thread means responsible risk-taking.

At a time of rampant social disconnection, a big shift towards renewed connectivity is beginning to emerge. We are awakening to the ancient truth that all human beings are purposefully interconnected with each other and with all living things and living systems. Both Western and Eastern perspectives converge upon the recognition that we are all constructed from the same basic ingredients, the same essential energy. Like intermingled parts of a global mind, we are completely linked with everything.

Midlife repacking can only occur by daring to act upon this reality and forging stronger connections where it counts: in our relationships, in our creative lives, and in our spiritual essences. And we have to do it in real time — not later today, not tomorrow, but now. The cost is not insignificant; the payoff, though, is incalculable. As the novelist Graham Greene wrote in *The Heart of the Matter,* "One small act of daring can change one's entire conception of what is possible."

Having A Midlife Crisis on Purpose

The midlife crisis, which we prefer to call the "midlife inventure," presents us with an opportunity to reexamine our lives and to ask the sometimes frightening, always liberating question: "What's next?"

In a coaching practice over the last three decades that has been predominately composed of people in midlife, Richard has seen the pattern again and again. The "midlife inventure" represents a turn within; a wonderful, though often painful, opportunity to reimagine our lives.

The Gospel according to Thomas states: "If you bring forth what is within you, what you bring forth will save you. If you do not bring forth what is within you, what you do not bring forth will destroy you."

Many people are designing new workstyles, "bringing forth" new views of the good life, new definitions of success. Success has different meanings at different ages and stages of life.

Richard relates a story he calls "Mind the gap" which reminds us how critical "bringing forth" is to our ability to navigate life's inevitable transitions:

> On the flight to London recently I sat next to a businessman. He irritated me by talking on his mobile phone loud enough for the entire cabin to hear. We had the sort of short conversation you get when you sit next to me. When the talk turns to small, mine vanishes. I'm not a talker on airplanes. I write or read.
>
> After takeoff, the fellow made a valiant attempt to engage me, but I was up to the challenge with my truthful decline, "I'm sorry; I have a deadline to meet." My response forced him to unpack his computer and play solitaire.
>
> Later, as the plane was taxiing to the gate, he asked me the standard traveler's question, "So what do you do?" He had been frustrated by my absorption in my writing. "I'm an author," I replied, giving him the partial truth.
>
> "I knew it!" he said. "I knew you were somebody!"
>
> Keeping with convention, I asked him the standard question, as well. "And what do you do?" "I'm having a midlife crisis," he

said, smiling painfully. "I'm 55 years old, just got downsized, and I'm wondering what I'm going to do with the rest of my life."

As we walked together down the moving walkway at London's Heathrow Airport, I heard the familiar recording "Mind the Gap!" reminding pedestrians to be cautious crossing the transition space between the moving and stationary footpaths. It struck me that my fellow traveler was facing a gap that is equally familiar to many people nowadays: the gap between what we had hoped for in life and how they have actually turned out.

Navigating this gap — essentially the space between our dreams and reality — is especially difficult because most of us have had scant preparation for doing so. Most of us have more or less followed a script written by someone else, a generic script that typically overlooks our unique talents and passions.

To write our own scripts, we need to ask ourselves questions that enable us to bridge the gap between where we've come from and what we're doing.

First, ask "What does success mean to me?" "I want to be somebody" is not an answer. What does being a "somebody" entail, anyway? Is the term a substitute for freedom and creativity? A more fruitful inquiry would be to explore a clearer conception of the good life, expressed in terms of "living in the place I belong, with people I love, doing the right work, on purpose."

Second, ask "What parts of my life are non-negotiables?" What values are constant? Knowing what we stand for — our non-negotiables — makes our choices about the way forward more consistent with who we really are and want to be.

Third, ask "What makes me want to get up in the morning?" Each of us is born with a purpose and a sacred duty to fulfill its promise. Clarity of purpose — knowing what difference we want to make in the world — enables us to make choices that more accurately reflect our innermost natures.

But because so few of us routinely ask — and answer — these questions, we find ourselves to be a society of notoriously numb people — lonely, bored, dependent individuals who are happy only when we have killed the time we are trying so hard to save.

We worry constantly about making a living, but rarely about making a life. In our businesses and financial markets across the country, people scramble frantically trying to make a killing, but end up instead killing their lives.

The vast majority of people endure their jobs because they see no other way to make a living. In addition, their work organizes, creates routine and structures their lives. At the very least, most jobs force us into a rhythm of weekend leisure, Monday's blues, Wednesday's "humpday," Friday's T.G.I.F., and regular paychecks. Our minds and bodies become so attuned to these rhythms that they become part of our own internal clocks. We forget that there are other ways of spending time or saving it to do the things and be with the people we love. We forget that there are other pathways that lead out of the wilderness, away from the rat race.

A Path Through the Wilderness

Psychologists know that the capacity for growth depends on one's ability to internalize and to take responsibility. If we only see our life as a dilemma that others have created, a problem to be "solved," then no change will occur. If we have a failure of nerve, no repacking can occur.

Conversely, if we view our life as a product of our own reimagining — as a mystery to be discovered — then we tend to remain flexible and open to new input all the time. If we're willing to take risks and face new challenges, we can continually recreate ourselves to meet the changing circumstances of our ever-unfolding experience.

The invitation to reimagine is a summons to become aware (unpack our bags), accept responsibility (repack our bags), and risk the journey of life to which we are called.

Daniel Boorstin, in his monumental book, *The Discoverers,* documents that medieval geographers and theologians blocked the exploration of new worlds for centuries by their refusal to use the ancient term "*terra incognita*" —"unknown land"— to describe places on their maps where people had not been. They preferred simply not to include those places at all. They found it safer to limit their depiction of the world than to face the fact that much of it was unknown.

Any adventure is also an "inventure." In order to seek out new lands and go where no person has gone before, one must first take a journey to the heart, the mind, and the soul.

To travel to that place we call "the good life" requires a similar inventure. We must survey territory we're searching for, and map out a route to get there. This type of planned inventure is the opposite of unconsciously acting out the patterns or paths of our past.

Inventuring requires the willingness to acknowledge the "*terra incognita*" quality of what we do not know. Inventurers celebrate the unknown and appreciate the unknown wilderness in their own spirit. Naturalist Eliot Porter proclaimed that "in wilderness is the preservation of the world." We see midlife inventuring as the preservation of the world within.

Each of us is trying to express more fully who we are. Each of us has a unique path through the wilderness. There is something meaningful — and even holy — in our diversity.

Without uncharted land, *terra incognita,* the process of living would lose much of its vitality and meaning. An inventuring life finds aliveness at the edges of discovery and growth. Some people naturally seem to live this way. Most of us have to work at it.

A middle-aged man in a recent workshop had spent several years making the transition from being laid off as the head of a staff department in a private corporation to teaching at a small liberal arts college. In that time, he went through several cycles — working on an advanced degree, taking a half-time job with a friend who was building a new business, simplifying his day-to-day financial needs.

In this workshop he talked about his future. He had tears his eyes. "Some people when they realize they are about to die say, 'Oh, shit!' I'm not going to be one of those. I'm taking the risk now to create the second half of my life. I finally got it — there is a difference between success and fulfillment. I had success, but I wasn't fulfilled. Maybe success is getting what you want. Fulfillment, though, is wanting what you get. And I didn't end up wanting what I got!"

The feeling that this man had — that of losing one's center — is familiar to anyone who has dealt with demands of external success while trying to fulfill internal values and needs. For those who try though, Kierkegaard may offer solace, "To venture causes anxiety; not to venture is to lose oneself."

Celebrating the Explorer Within

Richard admits, "The thrill of inventuring is consistently re-awakened in me when I visit Africa. Africa helps me understand and connect all aspects of myself. It causes me to open my eyes and see how I fit in. I am myself and everyone else too."

Every culture in one form or another celebrates the explorer who ventures, who experiences the world, confronts the unknown, and returns with the stories of their experience to enrich the community. The exploration process, often called the vision quest, takes on new significance since it brings us to a fundamental understanding of our true calling.

The inventure life is a life of continual repacking. Inventuring means we're willing to try on a wide variety of work options in order to develop a vision that reflects our true calling. This isn't an intellectual head trip. It's not spiritual pilgrimage just for the sake of it. It isn't latching on to every hip new philosophy that comes down the pike.

Rather, it's a result of practice — regular, daily practice. The practice may include being in nature, meditating, praying, playing music, drawing, sculpting, traveling, or simply spending time alone. All of these are ways to open our true calling.

Through such practice, we eventually realize a whole different level of aliveness. We come to feel our calling.

Oliver Wendell Holmes said, "Most people go to their graves with their music still inside them." Many people live their entire work lives and go to their graves never finding out who they wanted to be when they grew up.

Getting Here from There

Repacking is a cradle-to-grave process. It's something we need to go through again and again in our lives to sustain a feeling of aliveness at whatever age we are. The good life isn't something we can get and keep — it's an ongoing process of reinventing what it means to live in the place we belong, with the people we love, doing the right work, on purpose.

We can, however, at any time in our lives, design our lives so as to be living our vision of the good life at that time. The key to this is a conscious awareness about what we're carrying and why we're carrying it. One person who has managed to develop the reinventing awareness — and fairly early in life, all things considered — is Richard's son, Andrew Leider. Even as he began taking his first few steps into "adulthood," Andrew decided to try to live his vision of the good life, rather than find himself years later dreaming of or having regrets about what he never did when he had the chance.

At 23, Andrew chose to live in the right place — Red Lodge,

Montana — with people he loved, doing the right work — he was an Outward Bound Instructor — on purpose. Friends and former college roommates envied the choices he'd made. He said: "They tell me, 'I wish I were doing something like you're doing, but I couldn't take the time. I saw an opportunity and felt I just had to take it in this job market.'"

Andrew compared their situation to his own — a situation he designed by regularly asking himself the "why am I carrying this?" question.

> Most of my friends are driven by their current visions of the good life, just like I am. But they're already strapped to cars, apartments, furniture, and loans. Within the next five years, most will probably be married, have kids, and be well on their way, while I'll probably still be traveling in the mountains. If you're driven to a 5th Avenue lifestyle, then you won't be happy until you get there. But I'm not.
>
> For now, "right work" is what I'm doing. I love the process of working with others, as a team, to affect people's lives. I like working on hard questions. With Outward Bound I definitely feel a part of something important. People work here for a common purpose. We share a lot of the same values. We all seem to like doing things in unique ways. I guess that's why we all enjoy experiential learning. The purpose and values of that learning are more important than where it takes place . . . as long as it's outdoors.
>
> Minneapolis is the place I know best, where I grew up. But home, now, I feel I can create wherever I am. I'm not settled yet. I live in four separate worlds — my family, my few college friends I have chosen to stay connected with, my Red Lodge local friends, and my extended Outward Bound family. Home is not one place. It's the way I feel wherever I happen to be. I'm

trying to put as much joy into wherever I am and with whatever
I currently have.

Andrew summed up his early vision of the good life:

> My needs are pretty minimal. I don't have financial desires . . .
> yet! I have what I want — time and good work. I can get by with
> very little. It costs to live; it costs to get sick; it costs some to
> do the things I love to do outdoors. I want to keep enough in
> savings so I can take care of myself and still have time. That's the
> good life to me, now.

Andrew's vision of the good life evolved as he did. He chose to
move to Durango, Colorado and take a job that allowed him to develop his experiential learning skills in new arenas. As Director of *On
the Edge,* a firm doing action learning programs with corporations and
schools, he repacked his work bags and his place bags. He purchased
six acres of land with the goal of creating a simple, natural, outdoor-
based lifestyle. Andrew's financial desires increased, but he continued
to do a good deal of soul-searching about the question, "How much
is enough?"

Eventually, Andrew moved on from Durango to become Executive Director for Montana Yellowstone Expeditions, a non-profit
organization with a summer program for kids that combined an *Outward Bound*-type experience with core life skills. He bought a home
in Bozeman with his wife Cari Hanson and settled in for five years.
Again, the "thread" he was following continued to involve his love of
the outdoors with his passion for experiential education.

Recently, Andrew and Cari moved to San Francisco, California
to chart a fresh course as Program Director for the Golden Gate
Institute, an organization whose mission is to advance environmental preservation and global sustainability by facilitating cross-sector
dialogue and collaboration, encouraging new partnerships, and pro-

moting action. Once more, even in a new place, with a new job, the thread is maintained. Andrew's vision of the good life remains clear.

What is the good life to you, now?

Is your vision as clear as Andrew's? Do you know what you're carrying and why you're carrying it? Or is it time to think some more about unpacking and repacking?

Dave's Repacking

In the spring of 1991, I had an epiphany. On a lark (or perhaps it was the first robin of an incipient midlife crisis), I had decided to take an *Introduction to Philosophy* course at the University of Minnesota. This was my initial exposure to "real" academia since my undergraduate career careened off-course in the late 1970s. It was a lovely April evening, but I was trapped inside, in a small classroom, far off in the corner of an aging and no longer ivy-covered hall on the Twin Cities' campus. Around me, my classmates, all ten to fifteen years younger than me, slumped in their chairs or stared unblinkingly out the window as if by sheer willpower they could keep the sun from setting for two more hours — until class would be over — so as not to lose a single moment of light for roller-blading or skateboarding. At the front of the room my instructor, a grad student, was splitting hairs and casting pearls as he explicated the finer points of the teleological argument in David Hume's *Dialogues Concerning Natural Religion*. In contrast to the torpid ambience, his words, quickened by Hume's brilliance, flowed with a passion that would have seemed indelicate if it were not so authentic.

And suddenly, it occurred to me that I had come home.

The word "vocation" comes from the Latin *vocare*, a summoning, a calling; my instructor's voice was summoning me back home, to my true vocation, to my original calling — the study of philosophy.

So began a repacking that included resuming my 20-year mission to seek out and find an undergraduate degree — and eventually, to teach philosophy at the college level. I can't say that the studies have always been easy, or even all that intriguing. Balancing the demands of making a living with the need to read esoteric philosophical texts wasn't always a barrel of laughs. But it's been what I've needed to do. I took off a term when things got too intense, and I found that I didn't feel whole. I felt as if I was off track from where I was headed . . . not that I've always been clear about where that place is.

What I have discovered, though, and what this book in no small way represents, is that I'm finally becoming the person I've always been.

For most of my life, I was trying to be someone. After repacking, I finally learned that the real art is in letting myself reveal to the world the person I am.

The repacking I continue to be engaged in has involved several choices:

- Devoting less time to jobs for which I get paid, in order to allow myself time to do the work I need to for my own mental and emotional well-being.

- Making do with fewer "things" so as to have the experiences — educational and otherwise — that I want.

- Learning to say "no" to other people in order to say "yes" to myself.

- Deepening the existing relationships in my life, as opposed to widening my circle of new relationships.

- Finding beauty and satisfaction within, rather than always looking for the next "best thing" that's out there.

- Taking the long view, learning patience.

I've come to see the repacking experience I've gone through — and continue to go through — as a kind of blessing. And I've tried to express my gratitude for this blessing through my day-to-day activities in the world — including, of course, writing this book with Richard.

And who says you can't ever go home?

The Two Deadly Fears

Nowadays what most people feel when they don't feel anything in particular is fear.

It's easy to see why. The world is a frightening place. Certainly, the popular media do nothing to disabuse us of the notion. Television, movies, radio talk shows all remind us to be scared, very scared. It's as if we're being told that the one natural emotion to feel is a sort of vast, overriding, and persistent sense of fear.

Our investigations have revealed that though people are indeed fearful, their fear isn't really that vague. In fact, it can be broken down into two main fears, fears which we call the Two Deadly Fears because they sap so much of life out of all of us.

These Two Deadly Fears are:

1. Fear of Not Having Enough
2. Fear of Not Being Enough

You may be surprised that fear of death isn't at the top of the list. But it turns out that people aren't as afraid of death as you might expect. In fact, it's said that most people are more afraid of public speaking than they are of dying! Consequently, it's not all that strange really that the two we've identified seem to generate more chills than the mere prospect of death.

The Fear of Not Having Enough emerges naturally from our innate needs for safety and security. Obviously we have to meet the basic requirements for food and shelter before we can do anything else in our lives. But in a way, the Fear of Not Having Enough puts us on "overdrive" in our efforts to meet them. We become so fearful that they won't be attended to that we overdo it. The need for food, for instance (even when it's not at all an issue), gives rise to the fear that we won't ever have enough. Before we know it, we have a kitchen pantry filled with boxes and boxes of stuff we've picked up "just in case" that we'll never use, which end up being more of a burden to us than any real comfort. The Fear of Not Having Enough tends to make us grasp for more than we can handle in our lives, and consequently prevents us from realizing and embracing all we really need to be happy and fulfilled.

"The Fear of Not Being Enough" is the dread that we'll go to our grave having never made our mark, having never "sung our song." It's the scary feeling that keeps many of us hard at work, often in professions and projects that overwork us. And yet, ironically, it's often these very livelihoods, and the responsibilities associated with them, that keep us from ever allowing ourselves to really live.

The Fear of Not Being Enough can fuel our attempts to infuse our lives with purpose. If we can devote ourselves to a cause or belief larger than ourselves, we can — in some small way — achieve a slice of immortality. But again, as long as we keep seeing purpose as something "out there," instead of something generated from within, we never really achieve an authentic experience of the life that we have.

Thus, "achieving" the good life is, in a very real way, a matter of reconciling ourselves to and eventually, overcoming these Two Deadly Fears. To do that we must clarify our own authentic vision of what "living in the place I belong, with people I love, doing the right work, on purpose" means to us. And that, perhaps surprisingly, requires us not only to embrace this new vision, but often to let go of old ones.

At some level, all fear is fear of the unknown. When we consider repacking we must revisit the two great fears, "What if I don't have enough?" and "What if I am not enough?"

Unfortunately, there's really no way to answer these questions except through experience.

In order to overcome our fear of the unknown, we have to get to know it. Doing so is definitely scary, but it's the only way we'll ever *not* be frightened.

Dave says, "When I was a little boy, I used to lie in my bed at night, staring at the closed curtain of my bedroom window, terrified by the knowledge that behind the curtain, a leering space alien lay in wait for me. I dared not open it for fear of seeing his terrible green and grizzly, multi-eyed face. So I'd just lie there, stock still, working myself up into a state of stark terror. Eventually, I became so paralyzed with fear that I couldn't do anything other than whimper softly and hope my parents somehow heard me over their TV set. It wasn't until much later — probably when I was about 14 or so and started leaving my bedroom window open so my friends could sneak in at night or I could sneak out — that it finally occurred to me how I could overcome my fear. I realized that I didn't have to live with it. I could dispel the fear any time it started to grow, just by pulling back the curtain."

Same for repacking. If the idea of it seems terrifying (and there's plenty of reason for it to) the good news is that doing it is the one sure way to make the fear go away. But does knowing this make it any easier? Probably not.

It certainly didn't for Albert Brooks' character in his delightfully dark comedy *Lost In America,* which even nearly three decades after its release, still rings true. In the movie, he and his wife give up their successful middle-class lifestyle to go touring around the country in a Winnebago motor home. As they set out on the road, the Steppenwolf song, "Born to Be Wild," blares over the soundtrack.

But Albert and his wife soon discover that for them, the freedom of the road isn't all it's cracked up to be. And after she loses the family "nest egg" gambling in Las Vegas, they have no choice but to start over from scratch. He gets a job as a school crossing guard and she takes an assistant manager position at a fast food joint. The upshot is that within a few weeks, they've returned to the city and are once again working at their old jobs — although at a significant reduction in salary.

But at least they didn't end up late in life, still dreaming about traveling down the wild blue highway, right?

What If I Get Lost?

When we make changes in our lives, even subtle ones, it's not unusual to feel a little lost at first. Consequently, when we engage in repacking, it can seem like we really have ventured into a *terra incognita*. Even if the changes are welcome, we may find ourselves groping a bit, searching for familiar landmarks that are no longer there. It can be scary and confusing, and it may make us question whether we've done the right thing. The challenge, therefore, is to find some level of comfort with the unknown. Often that can emerge when we take the long view and recognize that where we are in life fits into a larger pattern.

This doesn't mean, of course, that we won't ever feel lost, but it does suggest that it may not be as difficult to find ourselves as we fear.

Dave tells a story that relates to this, in which he recalls the feeling of being lost.

> When I was a little boy, my mother's standard response when I whined that I had nothing to do was that I should "go get lost in the woods." She was kidding, of course, and never imagined that her only son might take her suggestion literally. But one day, I did.
>
> I set out from home about ten in the morning and marched straight into the suburban forest that bordered our housing development. In less than three hours I was hopelessly lost. I had no idea where home was and no sense at all about which way led back.

I ran around in circles, retracing the same pathways over and over. I remember passing a particular stand of blackberry bushes about six times from half a dozen different directions and feeling like I was doomed to repeat my steps for all eternity. Although there was little chance that I might disappear forever in this two or three square miles of well-domesticated woods, it seemed to my seven year-old brain that this was it. I would never escape. They'd find my bones, gnawed clean of flesh by raccoons and woolly worms.

After another hour or so of frantic searching, I finally found my way into a clearing that led to a hilly pasture. I ran ahead and came face to face with a horse. Terrified and relieved all at once, I burst into tears. My cries attracted the attention of the horse's owner, a kindly older gentleman who owned the hobby farm on which I was now trespassing. He calmed me down, dried my tears, and took me into his house so I could call my mom.

I remember his kitchen perfectly — the dusty light, the smell of baking, the warmth of the hot oven. It had a great big wooden table, just like all farmhouses are supposed to have. His wife, straight from Central Casting's farm-wife department, wore a flowered house dress and gave me freshly-baked cookies as fast as I could eat them.

Of course, by the time my mom showed up, I didn't want to leave. After receiving an invitation from my hosts to come back anytime though, I agreed to depart. In the car, driving home, Mom asked me why in heaven's name I had found it necessary to take her words at face value and actually go get lost in the woods.

Naturally, I said that I wasn't lost, that I had never been lost, and that my adventure had been planned right from the start. Mom just smiled and kept on driving.

The lesson here, I think, is that sometimes, when we're lost, we don't think we are. But also, sometimes, when we think we're lost, we're not.

As you repack your bags and set out on the next part of your life's journey, you may often feel lost. If so, it may be worthwhile to take a moment and consider if you really are — or if you're just retracing your steps in the forest on your way to somewhere new. On the other hand, it's also valuable to look around if you feel particularly sure of where you are. You may discover that you're deeper in the wood than you think — and that might not be so bad. After all, there's always a chance that cookies are quite close at hand.

What To Do If You're Lost

A friend of ours, Sarah Carter, decided to give up her career as a mechanical engineer and return to graduate school to study architecture. Two weeks after enrolling she knew she'd made a horrible mistake. She missed her home, her job, her friends — everything. Talk about feeling lost. In just two weeks she'd gone from being a successful businessperson and homeowner to an impoverished college student living in a basement apartment.

Being a skilled outdoorsperson, though, Sarah did what any skilled outdoorsperson does in this kind of situation. She didn't panic. She didn't make any rash moves. She didn't start running around looking for some way, any way, out. Instead, she just sat tight. She conserved her energy and regrouped. She remembered to stand still and listen.

Above all, Sarah observed. She observed the situation around her. She considered her reaction to it. She tried to get to the root of the anxiety and find out where it was coming from. She gave herself time to figure out what her options were. What could she change? What couldn't she? What was worth holding on to? What might she just as well give up?

Ultimately, it took Sarah about six months — and several long weekend vacations — to find herself. But find herself she did. She ended up completing her architecture degree and eventually, opening up her own firm. Had she let herself freak out and quit school before she ever really got started, this never would have happened. Instead of feeling — as she does today — that she's found her calling and is living it, she'd be feeling more lost than ever in her former life as an engineer.

Of course, the problem for most of us is that we're too impatient. We get antsy when things aren't perfect. We want our lives to be the way we want them to be NOW! No waiting, no figuring things out.

So, if you're feeling lost after repacking — or even if you're worried about feeling lost as you consider repacking — the best thing to do is probably nothing. Sit tight. Look around. Feel how you feel. And don't forget to breathe.

Other Lost Souls

Robert Bly entitled a work of his prose poems after a line in a piece by the poet, Rumi, "What have I ever lost by dying?" Rumi's message is that with every time he dies and is reborn, he sees progress. For hundreds of thousands of years, he was a mineral, then for hundreds of thousands more, a plant, then an animal, and finally a human being. You don't have to believe in reincarnation to feel that this makes sense.

Every time you give something up, every time you repack — even if it doesn't work out as planned — there is progress. As long as you keep your eyes, ears, and heart open, there's something to be learned.

Michael Levy, a software engineer we know, shares with us his philosophy of change with regard to romance and work:

"You know what the WORST thing about losing a job or breaking up with a lover is?" he asks.

His answer: "You always get a BETTER one next time!"

That sure seems true to us. Lots of times, people put up with painful situations much longer than they need to. They're afraid to let go because they don't know what's coming next — if anything. But once they're out of them, a whole new world opens up. Freed from the baggage of past patterns, they're able to see a myriad of new possibilities. Their self-worth skyrockets. As a result, they tend to attract more and even better responses, and the process feeds on itself, opening up increasingly richer options all the time.

It's a bittersweet truth, but we see this all the time in older people who have recently lost their spouse. In the period immediately following the death, they feel lost and scared and are apt to spend a lot of time by themselves, hibernating and regrouping. But within a year or so, they have blossomed. You find them taking art classes, doing volunteer work, traveling the world. They look healthier, happier, and more alive than they have in years. For some individuals, the "worst" thing about losing their spouse is that they get a second chance to find themselves.

Lost (Re)Generation

None of these stories are intended to make light of what you may be feeling regarding your own repacking adventure. On the contrary, by telling of how people have found themselves when they thought they were lost, our hope is to let you know you're not alone. Most people, when they go through the repacking process, experience a significant period of adjustment. You don't just radically change your life one day and pick things up right where you left off the next.

You need to give yourself time to get used to the changes; to adapt, to get comfortable with what's new and different. You know how it is when you literally repack a bag — things have to settle to the bottom. It takes a while for the lumps to smooth out and for things to stop rattling around. Same with your life. It takes time for new perspectives and arrangements to feel natural. And there's nothing you can do about this, really. Time, like the people who work at the Department of Motor Vehicles, is one of those things in life that you just can't rush.

In fact, the solution, when things seem to be going too slowly, may be to slow them down even more.

Moratorium: Inspire Before You Expire

Take a moratorium. What is it? What purpose does it serve? What power does it bring into your life?

Nearly everyone wants a time-out. Almost everyone needs one eventually. And we're not talking about just an afternoon off. We're talking about a real moratorium — a spiritual time-out in the truest sense. The root of the word spirit means to "breathe life into." We can say, then, that a moratorium is the opportunity to step back, take a deep breath and breathe life into your own life. It's an aspiration to inspire before you expire.

Elisabeth Kübler-Ross has stated the case for moratoriums as eloquently as anyone. "It is the denial of death that is particularly responsible for people living empty, purposeless lives; for when you live as if you will live forever, it becomes too easy to postpone the things you know that you must do. You live your life in preparation for tomorrow or in remembrance of yesterday, and meanwhile, each today is lost."[13]

Our lives today are consumed by time. Growing numbers of people feel tired and overwhelmed. We now live in the United States of Exhaustion. No matter what we do for a living, we share a common fear — that the clock will tick away when we aren't looking, leaving us unfulfilled and with no time left to fulfill ourselves.

What would your life be like if you took a moratorium? Would your family and friends support you, or tell you stories of people who had deviated from the straight path and ended up penniless and unemployable?

The moratorium way of thinking about time involves a major lifestyle shift, one that the world is ripe to accept. People know that there must be a better way; they just can't exactly identify what it is. What's important, though, is that, as a culture, we are beginning to realize that there are not just one, but many paths through time. The more we look at how we live, the more we see old time barriers that no longer serve us, and can be removed.

Paths Through Time

There is no one-size-fits-all plan for taking a moratorium. Ultimately, you will find your own path through time by unpacking and repacking — clarifying the good life as you go.

Even the business community is beginning to realize that changes are necessary. Corporations are becoming aware that to stay competitive, they need to alter their perception of time and its relationship to productivity and fulfillment. The economic and social implications of a burnt-out or unfulfilled work force are profound.

Bowen H. "Buzz" McCoy was the first participant in a six-month-long sabbatical program adopted by the investment banking firm of Morgan Stanley. He wrote about his experience in a popular article for the *Harvard Business Review,* entitled "The Parable of the Sadhu."

> After my three months in Nepal, I spent three months as an executive-in-residence at the Stanford Business School and the Center for Ethics and Social Policy at the Graduate Theological Union at Berkeley. These six months away from my job gave me time to assimilate 20 years of business experience. My thoughts turned often to the meaning of the leadership role in any organization.[14]

During his moratorium, McCoy discovered that, in his words, "there is always time," a perspective shared by another well-known time-outer, Lamar Alexander, former president of the University of Tennessee. In his book *Six Months Off: An American Family's Australian Adventure,* he described his six-month hiatus from politics. It was inspired by a comment his wife made. She said, "We've got to get out of here . . . maybe for a long time, not just some vacation; and as far as we can get. We need to get together again as a family, and you need to think about what to do with the rest of your life."[15]

They found a house in Sydney, Australia. The kids enrolled in school and Lamar set about trying to "do nothing." He read books he hadn't read in 20 years, took long walks, contemplated his vision, and in general, broke up patterns he'd been living for years.

What did he learn? After two months of close living, he said, "I think we always loved each other, but we learned to like each other more . . . I suppose we'll look back on it ten years from now and remember the crocodiles and the snowy mountains, but the most important thing will be that we were important enough to each other to take the time to do it while we still could."

It doesn't have to be Nepal or Australia; it doesn't have to be six months, or even two. It does, however, have to be a "change in the game": a break-up and break-down of your usual patterns. We think the following example gives a pretty clear idea of what we mean.

Sally Leider's Moratorium

Sally Leider used to give herself totally to her work. Every day, she came home exhausted, with telephone calls and computer work still left to do. At the end of the work week she collapsed into the weekend, desperate for a rest before facing Monday morning.

A compulsive workaholic? No! Sally was a gifted teacher of gifted and talented students. She knows that higher-order thinking skills and creative problem-solving talents are essential in today's world, and she was committed to helping each of her students ignite the learning spark. She believes everyone is gifted because everyone has something unique to express — herself included. Still, even for her, time-outs were critical to her ability to stay inspired.

"I was very much on a high," said Sally, as she described a 6-month moratorium she took after 22 years of teaching. "I found that I had more energy and a better perspective on things as a result of the time-out. It helped me develop new competencies that I liked a lot."

Sally took six months to renew herself and finish her Master's Degree in Experiential Education. To give an experiential component to her own education, she spent a month trekking and doing field observations in Tanzania.

The closing section of her Master's Thesis summed up the benefit of this moratorium:

> If my life is a heroic quest, a journey during which I discover my purpose, then how can my life be an expression of what matters to me? How can I be a model of my concern for planetary biodiversity? Through my experiences in Africa . . . I have further clarified my personal and professional commitment to confronting the biological diversity crisis.

She went on to say: "I always strive for new learning experiences. I hope there is reincarnation," she adds with a laugh, "because I would try other careers the next time around. I would probably teach for a while . . . then I might settle down and become a naturalist."

Several years earlier, Sally had taken a one-year moratorium to live in Mt. Shasta, California. It was the first time since she was three years old that she didn't go to school every day. She explained, "I had a deep intuitive feeling that I needed a major change. My mother had recently died, and it was a jarring wake-up call to me. I felt so alone, yet so free — like I had an unlimited choice in my life. I was more of a 'choice-maker,' seeing my life through a new filter.

"In Mt. Shasta, I was doing important 'inner business,' and I was inspired by the new people that I met. They seemed to be consciously living many of the values I valued. It was a great opportunity to re-discover what I really wanted. And what I really wanted was to come back to my roots.

"My strong sense of place drew me back to Minnesota — particu-larly the St. Croix River Valley. Like a homing pigeon coming back, I was pulled by instinct. I felt I belonged here."

Unless she had left, she would never have known where home was.

Louis Armstrong defined jazz: "I know it when I hear it, but I can't tell you what it is." In the same way, people like Sally know the need for a moratorium when they feel it, even if they can't tell you exactly how they'll do it. A moratorium gives them time to clarify their feel-ings and hear their inner music.

Sally summed it up: "Once you experience time-outs like this, you want to go back and do it again. After each one, I was on an emo-tional high for weeks. Thinking about this later, I figure that this feel-ing came from the daily freedom that allowed me an almost constant stimulation of new experiences, new challenges."

Sally has continued to seek new challenges and to reinvent her vision of the good life. She took a five-year mobility leave from teach-ing to explore her curiosity about how to help young people — especially young girls — face the choices and changes in their lives with confidence. She created a coaching practice called *Wild Indigo,* dedicated to the purpose of guiding girls and young women to "bloom naturally." She expanded her teaching into "watershed wisdom" in or-der to deepen her commitment to action on the environmental crisis. To complete her full-scale repacking, she also remarried and moved to the place she loves — the St. Croix River. Sally's moratorium gave her the space to clarify her vision and hear her inner music.

Your Own Moratorium

The person you've just read about chose to take a moratorium. Other people are forced to take time out for retraining or to start new careers. With millions of people regularly moving in and out of the work force, disengagement and re-engagement are becoming authentic survival skills.

Increasingly, professional obsolescence is forcing people back to school for re-tooling and retraining. Lifelong learning, as opposed to once-a-life learning, is becoming the norm.

Individuals and organizations are trying out all sorts of options — part-time work, part-time retirement, job-sharing, hour banks, flex-time, flex-place, retirement rehearsals, flex-year contracts, project-oriented working, telecommuting, sabbaticals. All kinds of moratoriums are emerging as real possibilities for more and more people. Some businesses even find it necessary to include moratoriums as part of their compensation packages in order to compete for the best and the brightest.

Shouldn't you do the same for yourself?

A Well-Lived Day

At some point, you may choose to take a chunk of your life's time to discover or experience a moratorium — new places, new relationships, new work or a new sense of purpose. Perhaps you'll end up "living in the place you belong, with the people you love, doing the right work, on purpose."

As we have talked with people about their moratoriums, many have told us that before they took theirs, the idea of doing so seemed impossible. Yet afterwards, emerging with a new life perspective, they wondered why they had waited so long. Sally Leider said that each day of her moratorium felt like a "well-lived day."

How often most go to bed at night saying "this was a well-lived day?" And if not, why not? How can we purposefully repack to ensure that we do?

Ujamaa

It is said that once Africa gets into your system, you will always return. No one knows this better than Richard.

He has been called back to the continent — specifically, Tanzania — for some three decades now, drawn, of course, by the wildlife and wilderness, but equally, by the Tanzanian people. They are the essential source of the pull to return, the "thread" he holds on to each time he visits. Among no other people has he found such a spirit of purpose; in no other place has he seen such willingness to help someone in need.

This is the quality known as *ujamaa*, (or alternately, *undugu*) which permeates Tanzanian society and blankets the country in emotional warmth. *Ujamaa* means "brotherhood." The word includes notions of extended family, generosity, and compassion towards others throughout the community and even beyond.

Ujamaa helps explain why manners in Tanzanian society are so highly valued, why handshakes are so full of affection, and why laughter is so irrepressible. It might also explain why the country remains a beacon of peace in Africa, why it opens its doors to so many refugees, and why it has historically eluded the power of a despotic ruler.

Ujamaa refers to the unspoken social safety net; the "haves" willingly share with the "have nots," and one person who has a job might support a dozen friends and relatives who don't. For most Tanzanians, it is inevitable that a long-lost "cousin" will eventually materialize and ask for work, money for an emergency, or a place to stay. And it is just as inevitable that the request will be granted.

Tanzanians are warm, friendly people who regularly welcome strangers with acts of enormous kindness. As a frequent visitor, Richard has received numerous offers of help from people with whom he's become friends, like Koyie, as well as from individuals he'd never met before — *ujamaa* in practice.

This spirit of *ujamaa* has much to teach us no matter where we are. If you live with a spouse, children, an aging parent, even a dog or a cat, you sometimes have to put their interests or needs ahead of your own. It's easy to resent the demands on our time and energy, but if we can embody a feeling of *ujamaa*, we're more apt to embrace the opportunity to help.

It turns out that *ujamaa* is an effective strategy for lightening the load. In addition to reducing social isolation, it also helps decrease the self-absorption that dulls one's vitality. Thus, it can lead to stronger feelings of purpose and meaning in our lives.

Since childhood we've been told that virtue is its own reward. In fact, research now shows that doing good for others brings very tangible benefits in terms of health and longevity. In his book, *The Healing Power of Doing Good,* former Peace Corps volunteer and community organizer Allan Luks introduced the term "helper's high" to describe the rush of good feeling — *ujamaa* — that people get when they do good for others. Since the book's publication, neuroscientists have learned that altruism activates the same centers in the brain involved in pleasure responses to food and sex.

From the study of over three thousand volunteers, Luks concluded that people who regularly volunteer to help others are ten times more likely to be in good health than those who don't. In a similar vein, the landmark Social Capital Community Benchmark Survey reported that those who gave contributions of time or money to causes in which they believe are 42 percent more likely to be happy than people who refrain from giving.

Sociologist and happiness expert, Dr. Christine L. Carter, writes: "People 55 and older who volunteer at two or more organizations have an impressive 44 percent lower likelihood of dying [prematurely] — and that's after sifting out every other contributing factor, including physical health, exercise, gender, habits like smoking, marital status, and many more. This is a stronger effect than exercising four times a week or going to church. It mean that volunteering is nearly as beneficial to our health as quitting smoking!"

It seems the Tanzanian people know something that others of us around the world are only beginning to discover: the spirit of *ujamaa*, of putting others first, is not only good for those that are helped; it's also highly beneficial for those who help.

By lightening the load for others we lighten the load for ourselves as well.

CHAPTER 7

The Freedom of the Road

What's It All About?

The theme song of the 1970s cult movie, *Alfie,* asks "What's It All About?" Think of the tune as an anthem for everyone who seeks a reason for being — a reason "to get up in the morning." In the face of bewildering change and endless transition, more people than ever before are hungry for a feeling that they matter. We find ourselves looking for what Viktor Frankl wrote about in *Man's Search for Meaning:* a clear sense of what we were put on this planet to do and to be.

As its title suggests, *Man's Search for Meaning* is written for anyone interested in what it means to live a meaningful life. In this classic work, inspired by his suffering and survival in the Holocaust, Frankl explains how anyone can find meaning in life, no matter what their circumstances, and why even a life of unbearable pain can be meaningful. In our current era of crisis and uncertainty, as people increasingly begin to reimagine their lives, Frankl's work seems newly relevant.

Frankl writes eloquently of what he calls "tragic optimism," the human condition in which we all find ourselves as we realize that life inevitably brings pain, guilt, and death, and yet, for the most part, we still manage to carry on. It's a poignant example of life reimagined, as Frankl encourages us to turn suffering into achievement, relying on guilt to improve ourselves, and using the knowledge that life is short as a spur to meaningful action.

Half a century later, this sort of tragic optimism — often expressed as "resilience" — has become a key theme in the increasingly influential field of positive psychology, the study of the gifts and passions that enable individuals to live thriving and meaningful lives. Rather than focusing on self-esteem, regardless of achievement, positive psychology emphasizes the ability to be resilient in the face of life's setbacks — and for that matter, successes as well. This is perfectly consistent with Frankl's approach to the coping mechanisms he employed in order to survive his concentration camp experience. He found meaning in his experience of the Holocaust by taking the opportunity to not only observe others in unimaginably desperate situations, but also to reframe and make use of those insights himself.

Reimagining one's life means learning how to reframe information to find other ways of looking at our thoughts and options. In another of his books, *Man's Search for Ultimate Meaning,* Frankl gives the example of an older man devastated by the loss of his wife. The man is angry that she died first, leaving him alone and despairing in old age. Frankl advises him to reframe the situation and think of his living longer in different terms. The man has saved his beloved from experiencing the grief that he is now experiencing; he should consider reframing his loss as a gift to the person he adored most in the world.

Perhaps the part of Frankl's message most relevant to our book is his perspective on the challenge of living meaningfully. He often spoke of the choice between taking a job that pays well and one that brings your life meaning. For Richard, this particular dilemma has special relevance; in 1968, after meeting Frankl in person, he ultimately chose a lifework path of meaning.

In the "new normal" global climate of endless change and instability, Frankl's insights have lessons for us all. He was convinced that even when every bit of control appears to have been taken away from us (such as, in his case, when facing death in a concentration camp), it is still possible for human beings to find meaning. And although hopefully, none of us will ever experience such horror, we do know how it feels, in the contemporary world, to be subject to forces far beyond our control. The "existential vacuum" of modern life challenges us endlessly to seek out and find meaning. As we attempt to reimagine our lives in a time when isolation is increasing and trust is eroding, Frankl's advice resonates powerfully, as he encourages us to find shared meaning in a new sense of community and common purpose.

At its most basic level, Frankl's message is about compassion, a quality he embodied throughout his life. For instance, he had the opportunity to leave Vienna before the war, but chose to stay behind in spite of the risks, to care for his parents. His own tragic experiences could have led him to dismiss as trivial ordinary complaints about the meaninglessness of the safe lives most of us lead. Instead, he understood clearly that any of us can feel lonely, isolated, and hungry for meaning, no matter what our situation. As a consequence he put his insights into practice in his own life, by devoting himself to helping others embark on their own search for meaning. His aspiration for each of us was that we find our own way, and reimagine our own lives as meaningful.

We are drawn from Frankl's overall search for meaning into his deeper, more personalized question, from "What is the meaning of life?" to "What is the meaning of my life?" We might pose the question in two additional ways: "What gets you up in the morning?" And "What keeps you awake at night?" And then, of course, the all-important follow-up: "Are you fulfilling your life's purpose?"

Poet Mary Oliver asks it this way: "What will you do with your one wild and precious life?" How many among us are, indeed, living up to those wild and precious possibilities? How many are exercising their courage and curiosity on a regular basis?

This is pioneering territory. After all, no one really wants to live a totally wild and crazy life. That will only lead to suffering. And besides, we think, we're already living good lives. We're generous — at least with our families and friends. We care about making a difference in the world. We don't fail more than anyone else we know. We're good-hearted, and we're doing our best.

But still . . . could there be something more? Can we look a little deeper? What really is the "good life"? And how does it differ from just a pretty good one?

One thing is quite extraordinary: and that's how ordinary are most of the so-called good lives we've studied. The closer you look at these ordinary lives, the more extraordinary they appear.

Two American Dreams

There are two American dreams, and they seem diametrically opposed to each other. The first is about freedom, liberty, and the lure of the new frontier. The second is about safety, security, and a home of one's own. The first dream is about the excitement of the road. The second dream is about the security of the hearth.

Both versions of the dream have powerful appeal. Both are deeply ingrained in our national psyche. Together, both are the cake we eat and want to have, too.

Most of us constantly go back and forth between them. One moment, all we want is the sky over our heads and a quiet place for shelter. The next, we feel we've got to be looking at that sky through the skylight of a brand-new home.

We're told by millions of advertisements for thousands of products that we can have it all. But the fact is, many of us don't even know what "it" is!

For years, we've been asking people to define the "good life." No matter what their income, most say that if they only had twice as much as they currently have, they'd be set. They'd have fulfilled the promise of the Declaration of Independence — life, liberty, and the pursuit of happiness. But when they achieve that new level, they're still not fulfilled. It turns out they'd been pursuing unhappiness all along.

Ultimately, it all comes back down to a question of how to define the good life. What is it for you? Freedom or Security?

In Isak Dinesen's classic book, *Out of Africa*, Karen Blixen and Denys Finch-Hatton have a conversation that brings out the tension between freedom and security, between the desire to settle down and be married and the desire for the freedom of the road.

Karen confronts Denys with her knowledge that when he goes away, he doesn't always go on safari. He admits this is true, but insists that it's not meant to hurt her. She responds that nevertheless, it still does hurt, to which he replies:

> Karen, I'm with you because I choose to be with you. I don't want to live someone else's idea of how to live. Don't ask me to do that. I don't want to find out one day that I'm at the end of someone else's life. I'm willing to pay for mine, to be lonely sometimes, to die alone if I have to. I think that's fair.

Karen answers that it isn't fair at all. Because by his actions, he's asking her to pay as well.

And this, of course, is much of the struggle when it comes to resolving questions of freedom and security. None of us live in a vacuum. Our actions and attitudes are completely interconnected with the actions and attitudes of others. Unlike Denys Finch-Hatton, most of us find that the option simply to go away — whether on safari or not — does not openly present itself. Yet at the same time, Finch-Hatton characterizes, albeit to an extreme, what many of us yearn for in our lives. We're looking for a way to ensure that we don't end up living someone else's life. We're looking for new frontiers, new adventures, new places where — at least for a little while — we can feel free.

Unfortunately, most of us, in most of our working lives, are driven by deadlines. Product release dates. Fiscal year ends. Final notices. It's no wonder they call them "deadlines," because, as many people feel, it's deadlines that are killing them!

Is there any escape? We can't really put our foot down and bring everything to a grinding halt, can we?

In the conclusion of his masterpiece, *Walden,* Henry David Thoreau tells a story about an artist in the city of Kouroo who sets out to make the perfect walking staff. Understanding that into a perfect work, time does not enter, he says to himself, 'It shall be perfect in all respects, though I do nothing else in my life.' The artist then, in his ongoing quest for perfection, transcends time. By the time he has found the perfect wood for his staff and shaped it perfectly, eons have passed, leaving no mark upon him or his work. As he puts the finishing touches on his perfect staff, he sees that the lapse of time he once experienced was an illusion. In crafting perfection, he has entered a realm that time cannot touch.

In our own lives, when we let ourselves experience the perfection of the present, we do the same thing. When we're not exhausted by what has happened or worried about what's to come, we enter a realm outside — or more appropriately — inside of time. That's how we know we've found the right pace. We're neither ahead of ourselves or behind. That's what it means to balance the load — we're right where we are.

Balancing the four elements of the good life is how we shift our perspective to gain the freedom of the road. Because, as it turns out, it's not that most of us don't have enough time, it's that *we don't have enough of the kind of time we want.*

If you know where you want to spend your time — on work, love, place, or purpose — and can allocate it accordingly, you won't feel so trapped. You'll feel less weighed down by the demands of your schedule and more in control of where you are headed.

If you find you don't have enough time, there are basically two things you can do:

- Increase your income to "buy more time," or . . .
- Simplify your life to "own more time."

Duane Elgin points out in *Voluntary Simplicity:*

> We all know where our lives are unnecessarily complicated. We are all painfully aware of the distractions, clutter, and pretense that weigh upon our lives and make our passage through the world more cumbersome and awkward. To live with simplicity is to unburden our lives — to live more direct, unpretentious, and unencumbered relationships with all aspects of our lives: consuming, working, learning, relating and so on.[16]

Bureau of Honest Admissions, Department of Walking Your Talk

After making our pitch for simplicity, we as authors need to back up a little and admit that, after all, we both live well by nearly any socio-economic standard. We haven't any right — nor indeed, any inclination — to suggest that the good life is only to be achieved by divesting oneself of all one's possessions and making a career of living off alms. Far from it.

Our commitment is to regularly asking ourselves, "How much is enough?"

Simplicity is not a static condition that you can possess. It is an ever-changing art, the art of needing less and being more.

How to bring that art to fruition is a question to be asked over and over again throughout our lives.

Betrayed by Success

At some point in our lives many of us feel trapped. By the time we are in our late thirties or early forties, nearly all of us have become specialists in something — work, parenting, whatever. Because our specialties have consumed, and continue to consume, our time, the underdeveloped parts of ourselves become more obvious.

Carl Jung pointed out that by the time we are 40 or 50 or so, we are bound to feel that our lives are out of balance, merely because we have overfocused our time and neglected parts of ourselves. Our "undiscovered self" yearns to be discovered.

Some of us feel betrayed by our success. Our private thoughts reveal a conflict between staying on the current road or seeking a "road not taken" — a new life direction. We feel confused and unable to sort things out.

We go through our days looking in on our lives, aware that we are living on borrowed time, but unable to take a time-out and make changes.

In seminars and speeches, time and time again, people consistently come up to us with one issue. They say things like:

"I feel trapped. I'm bored beyond tears with what I do. I don't know how I can continue in my current job, but I can't (or won't for financial reasons) leave."

"I've reached a plateau in my career. I need to move on and test undeveloped talents."

"I need to realize some of my lifelong dreams — like climbing Mt. Kilimanjaro!"

And they go on to ask:

"I wish my job gave me more flexibility. How can I take a time-out?"

We encourage these questioners to be "Walter Mitty" — James

Thurber's famous "time-outer"—for awhile. The message of "The Secret Life of Walter Mitty" is not so much the humor of Mitty's mental time-outs, but that after each of his adventures, he settles back into his old life—only with a renewed sense of energy and perspective.

Many years of listening to people's midlife stories has convinced us how deeply people hunger for little time-outs. And how much good it does to take them.

Satisfaction always leads to dissatisfaction; that's human nature. It's very difficult to sustain a passion for something you've been involved in for many years—whether that's a job, a relationship, or a community. Success always becomes routine and mechanical; that's how it becomes success in the first place. So you have to reinvent yourself. You have to dream of something new to revitalize the old, original feelings of aliveness.

When the surprise goes out of life, the life goes out of life, too. You no longer experience the growth edge that got up in the morning with a smile. Time-outs, though, are wake-up calls on purpose. They give us that new sense of surprise and mystery about what today will bring.

Richard says it was Richard Bolles (author of the perennial bestseller *What Color Is Your Parachute?*) who first challenged him to question his assumptions about taking time out. In a dinner conversation, Dick Bolles confronted the craziness of compressing work into the middle years of our lives. He asked Richard, "Why don't you carve out chunks of your retirement along the way, instead of saving it all until the last years of your life?"

Richard decided to take Bolles' advice seriously. Since 1984, he has set a goal of traveling to places like Africa every year. He has led yearly treks there for three decades and has helped to create the Dorobo Fund for Tanzania to support conservation and leadership development projects.

Richard says, "If it hadn't been for Africa, I'm not sure I could have stayed all these years in this business. The time I take there each year gives me a context, a means to connect the separate parts of me into a whole. When I return, I never stop thinking of the images, not for a day. Even when it is not in my conscious mind, I can feel it somewhere. It is always there."

Bolles later went on to propose new ways of restructuring our lifestyles and workstyles in his book, *The Three Boxes of Life and How to Get Out of Them.* He noted that traditionally, life has been viewed as made up of three boxes — Education, Work, and Retirement.[17]

Because people tend to live longer these days and, in general, are more affluent than their forebears, a new lifestyle model is needed. Instead of seeing the "retirement" box as 20-some years of old age tagged onto the end of a 30-some-years long "work" box, we can scrap the three boxes and create a new model that is more flexible and fluid, and more in keeping with current realities.

Still, most people find it difficult to muster up the courage to say good-bye and let go of the traditional model. The path from childhood to old age is still a straight line for most of us. The forces of inertia and money keep us moving in one direction, with little room for pausing, regrouping, detouring, or taking time-outs.

It's no surprise, therefore, that many people feel isolated and alone, even while possessed of technology and systems meant to bring us all closer together.

The Age of Social Isolation

The Information Age has given us virtually unlimited access to facts, figures and data about nearly everything in the world; it has allowed for instantaneous networking among people and organizations all around the globe; it has streamlined communications in ways that would have seemed the stuff of science fiction barely a decade ago.

But has it led to closer, more authentic, more *human* connections among us? The answer is unclear. In fact, a strong case can be made that the Information Age has resulted in a world that is more fractured and individualistic than ever before. The Information Age, it can be said, has given way to what might be called The Age of Social Isolation.

These days, more and more of us are spending more and more of our time, both at home and at work, surfing the internet, texting and talking on mobile phones, attending to email, watching television, and being stimulated by other new media — all experiences that are relatively recent in their availability to human beings. And given that the widespread availability of such experiences correlates closely with an increased sense of stress and isolation for so many of us, one can't help but conclude that they represent another major challenge to living the good life.

Why is this? As we become more connected, we seem to simultaneously become more disconnected, more isolated. An increasing number of the connections we do make are virtual, via phone or computer, as opposed to the tangible, face-to-face interactions we are made for. And, at the same time, as our high-tech experiences increase, we reduce the number of high-touch opportunities, choosing instead to spend our time watching videos or playing games online, or indulging in the many forms of escape from human contact available through allegedly "social" media.

This type of social isolation undermines our emotional well-being. Though they're difficult to resist, resist we must in order to feel whole and truly connected with ourselves and others.

Richard has long been pushing back against the socially-isolating aspects of technology. He was an early resister of both email and mobile technology. As a life coach he often heard clients complain about having to be "on" 24/7 and how technology had hijacked the human moments in their lives.

Finding his own peace with technology has been an ongoing challenge for Richard, especially as it has increasingly become the preferred way of doing business and keeping in touch with friends and associates. He has effected a truce, if you will, by ensuring that the technology works for him, rather than the other way around. "I do email almost exclusively at my desk at work or at home," he says, "and almost never on my mobile phone or on the fly. I only check my messages at certain times during the day — usually at 10:00 a.m. and 2:00 p.m.; that's it. I almost never leave my phone on during meetings or while in restaurants or public places. It pains me to have to hear other people's mobile phone conversations in airplanes before takeoff, at coffee shops, or even — most pathetically — in restrooms. I honestly believe their lives would be better if only they'd restrict their use as I do. These days, I rarely let ringing phones capture my attention or even draw me away from what I'm doing — and I'm happier as a result."

Although everyone's lives are different and we all have different needs when it comes to our use of technology, there's much to be said for — and gained by — setting limits like Richard does. Dave routinely assigns students in his Environmental Ethics class the challenge of going a weekend without using a computer, mobile phone, videogame console, MP3 player, or other high-tech devices. While it's not uncommon for students to echo the words of one young man who said that he felt as if he was "in prison," many also tell him how liberating they found the experience. One young woman wrote, in her reflective paper, that for the first time in a long time she could actually "hear herself think."

Another effective antidote to 24/7 living is to cultivate silence. Many of us are unaware of how loud our lives are, and how the constant noise we experience affects our sense of calm and well-being. In his revealing book, *In Pursuit of Silence; Listening for Meaning in a World of Noise,* author George Prochnik tells of being on patrol in Washington, DC with a police officer named John Spencer, who explained to him that the majority of the domestic disputes he responds to these days are actually noise complaints. Spencer said:

"You go into these houses where the couple, or the roommate, or the whole family is fighting, and you've got the television blaring so you can't think, and a radio on top of that, and somebody who got home from work who wants to relax or sleep, and it's obvious what they're actually fighting about. They're fighting about the noise. They don't know it, but that's the problem."

Before he even lets the combatants explain why they're fighting, Spencer routinely has them turn down the music and television, and switch off the game station, and just sit there for a minute. "You'd be amazed," he says, "how often that's the end of it."

Think about the disputes in your own life, not just with others, but also within yourself. How many of these are the product of just too much noise? How many could be resolved by just cultivating a few moments of silence?

Reboot Your Life

Finding meaning through the busy routines of work and life is not easy.

Many of us are afflicted with what can be called "hurry sickness": the feeling that there's too much to do, that we can't possibly slow down, that we'll never catch up and get done what needs to be done. Hurry sickness — always going somewhere, never being anywhere — is numbing our conscious awareness of what is happening in and to our lives.

Our very sense of humanity — our full presence in our own lives — is being hijacked by busyness.

Our daily routines often lack a sense of purpose, and appear to serve no apparent end. To find that sense of meaning and purpose we need to *reboot* our operating systems and see beneath the surface, to a place where we can experience authentic knowing — not with the mind, but with the heart.

David Levy, a professor in the Information School at the University of Washington, created a video called "No Time to Think," that brings this point home in stark relief. The video offers a disturbing wake-up call, showing how American society has become enslaved to an ethic of "more-better-faster," and is losing the capacity for reflection and presence. Levy's research focuses on why the technological devices — computers, smartphones, and so on — that are designed to connect us also seem to disconnect us.

A technology like Twitter may be the next level of connection, but surely there is something strange and ironic about the acceleration of Twittering as our human moments of presence dwindle. Instead of connecting us, our devices are isolating us.

And this isolation is becoming the norm.

Email, voicemail, instant messaging, mobile phone, text messaging, Facebook, Twitter, and of course the World Wide Web all serve useful roles.

But these tools for connecting also crowd out our moments of deeper purpose and relationship.

According to Thomas Eriksen of the University of Oslo, author of *Tyranny of the Moment,* the digital environment favors "fast-time" activities — those that require instant, urgent responses. The right-now is trumping the timeless — high-tech is hijacking high-touch. Such activities tend to take precedence over and shut out "slow-time" activities, such as reflection, play, and "courageous conversations."

And, as a result, we are becoming numb and fatigued. Deep-down, behind-the-eyeballs fatigued.

A remedy for this is to *reboot* — to reset our internal operating systems.

One effective way to reboot is to take a 12-hour "media fast"— a time during which you turn off all technology.

When we take a media fast, we unmask illusions. We confront what parts of our busyness are expressions of our real purpose.

When we lose touch with our core, we lose perspective on our purpose. We gain back our perspective by turning off technology and by letting our intuitive voice guide us.

Sometimes we are open to rebooting; at other times we are not. When crises drop into our lives, we are forced to reboot. At times when things seem to be going smoothly, we may not sense the need at all.

But the truth is: "pay now or pay later." Failing to stop and take stock of our lives now inevitably results in things getting away from us later. Taking a media fast may seem strange, yet it can help us pay now. It can enable us to connect more meaningfully not only with others, but also with ourselves.

When we're connected to everyone, we don't really know anyone. In order to know people, we have to listen to their stories.

But we live in an age when we rarely take time to hear each other's stories.

So, we live on assumptions.

We're busy people, after all, and we want our friendships easy and stress-free.

To counteract this, take a media fast — go without media or gadgets for 12 hours!

No mobile phone, computer, TV or radio for 12 hours. A break from techno-busyness forces us to confront core questions about life.

Questions like:

- "Do I see friends enough?"
- "Do I really know their stories?"
- "Am I accessible to them?"

On the morning of your media fast, try to get up a little earlier than usual.

Before you get involved in anything, just sit quietly for ten minutes and take three deep breaths.

First breath: be present.

Second breath: be grateful.

Third breath: decide to make a positive difference in one person's life, today.

Then envision your next twelve hours.

Picture the activities of the day without technology.

Picture the potential "purpose moments"—times you might make someone else's life just a little bit—or even a lot—better.

Throughout the day, look for those purpose moments—opportunities to connect with people through a question, a kind word, an extended hand.

In the purpose moments, ask people what they are truly excited about, passionate about, a learning adventure that was exciting for them—and listen.

What is the mood of these purpose moments?

Typically, it's one most of us yearn for—the feeling that there's someone in our lives who cares.

Whether we're aware of it or not, most of us want someone to push the pause button on technology and listen to our stories. We're hungry for deep connection.

The essence of rebooting is captured clearly by William Deresiewicz in an essay entitled *Faux Friendship*. He writes, "Exchanging stories is like making love. It is mutual. It is intimate. It takes patience, devotion, sensitivity, subtlety, skill—and it teaches those qualities too."

Rebooting our operating systems is powerful.

It slows us down to the speed of the story.

It teaches us that patience, devotion, sensitivity, subtlety, skill, and sharing are fundamental qualities to finding meaning in a stressed-out world.

In other words, it helps us find ourselves, right where we belong.

A Vacation From Words

Having successfully completed a "media fast," you may want to take it to the next step — a full-on "vacation from words."

The average adult American speaks approximately 5000 words a day. And the more successful we become, the more talking we tend to do. Words come spilling out of us, often with great intensity. We have so much to say, there's never time to listen — not to anyone else, and certainly not to ourselves.

That's a why a 24-hour "mini-vacation" from words at your favorite listening point can be so significant. A vacation from words provides a unique way to experience self-renewal. It's an opportunity to unpack everything for a brief period, even in the face of overwhelming busyness. It's a chance to find a new reason for getting up in the morning — or rediscover an old one.

A 24-hour retreat to your listening point allows the truth to creep back into your life. It enables you to ask yourself, "What is this situation I'm in (or person I'm involved with) trying to teach me?" And above all, it provides you the space you need to really hear the answer.

Following are ten points you may choose to reflect on in your listening point. Some of these are ideas touched on in other parts of this book. Others are issues we've found useful to think about during our own periods of reflection. In either case, we encourage you to find time at your listening point to take a vacation from words and consider one or more of the items listed here. You don't have to talk about these with anyone — just listen.

Repacking Reflections

1. **Rediscover your hidden talents.**

   Life at its source is about creating. Talents are the creative core of your life. What are you creating? Are you expressing your talents fully? If not, how can you?

2. **Reclaim your purpose.**

   Talents develop best in the crucible of purpose. When you're using your talents in support of something you truly believe in, you feel more energetic, more committed, and more enthusiastic about everything you do. Have you reclaimed your purpose? If not, what can you do to own it?

3. **Reinvent your job.**

   Satisfaction always leads to dissatisfaction. Most things repeated over and over become mechanical. Even the things we love best become stale if we don't renew them regularly. Are you regularly reinventing your job? Are you continually looking for new problems to solve, new ways to add value? How can you reinvent your job so you get up every morning (or at least most mornings) excited about the prospects ahead?

4. **Re-elect your personal board of directors.**

   Most of us can trace our successes to pivotal support from other people. What are the important relationships that have sustained you along the way? Who are the people in your life that you've relied on for counsel and advice? Think of them as your own personal board of directors. Picture yourself at a board meeting with these people. You're all around the table. Who sits at the head? Do you? As you sit there, right now, what issues would you like to bring before the board? How would you like them to react and what kind of support are you looking for?

5. **Re-sharpen your growth edge.**

   If the rate at which you're learning is not equal to or greater than the rate of change today, you'll soon be obsolete. Just like a successful company, you need to engage in serious Research & Development activity. Research new opportunities. And develop new skills. Learning brings aliveness. What are you excited about learning? How can you continually sharpen your growth edge?

6. **Repack your relationship bags.**

   Many of us, even in our deepest, most personal relationships, figuratively have a bag by the door, partially packed. Consider the primary relationships in your life. Are you and your loved ones having "radical conversations"? Does it feel like you're creating a "grand dialogue"? The number one cause of relationship problems is suppressed communication. How can you fully unpack with your loved ones and open the door for deeper, more meaningful communication?

7. **Reframe your time boundaries.**

   Sit down with your calendar and your checkbook. Review how you're spending two of your most valuable currencies — your time and your money. Are you satisfied with where your time and money are going? When was the last time you went to sleep at night saying, "this was a well-spent day"? Are you consistently saying "no" to the less important things in your life and "yes" to your real priorities?

8. **Rewrite your own vision of the good life.**

   The self-fulfilling prophecy is the surest of all — if you can dream it, you can do it. Beware of waking up sometime in the future and finding out that you've been living someone else's vision of the good life. Look forward. Dream a little. How do you "declare victory"? What does success really look like to you?

9.　**Reflect daily.**

Are you "always going somewhere; never being anywhere"? Have you succumbed to the "hurry sickness" so common in to-day's society? If your brain is always filled with the noise and chatter of modern living then you're exhibiting the symptoms. If your heart and mind feel numb, then you know you've got it. The antidote: regular time-outs. Mini-vacations. Appointments with yourself. Even fifteen minutes or so a day can work won-ders. Have you found a regular time and place to be alone, to put yourself on your own daily calendar?

10.　**Rediscover your smile.**

The average person smiles fifteen times a day. Does that seem like a lot or a little to you? Are you having fun yet? Are you experienc-ing real joy? Fun and joy are different. Fun is an outer expression, joy is an inner glow. Joy is derived from a harmony among place, love, work, and purpose. Are you feeling more or less joy in your life than you did last year at this time? Why or why not?

Everything Old Is New

Life is nothing else than a dynamic process. It's impossible to some-how find and catch happiness, because as soon as you trap it, it begins to wither. That's actually what repacking is all about — it's a system for helping you with the continuing search. No matter what form that system takes, it has to come from within.

In the 17th century the philosopher Benedict de Spinoza engaged in his own repacking. He began by considering the efforts involved in pursuing what most people esteemed as the highest good — riches, fame, and the pleasure of senses. Spinoza concluded that, while these had their attractions, they could never provide him with the authen-tic happiness for which he was searching. He made a great discovery, which he phrased as follows. "Happiness or unhappiness is made wholly to depend on the quality of the object which we love." If we love fleeting attractions and transitory values, our happiness will be fleeting and transitory as well. On the other hand, if we seek to fix our love to longer-lasting values, our happiness likewise tends to persevere.

Spinoza laid down three principles for how to carry on his life in a manner that would permit him to engage in his ongoing search for what really mattered to him. In summary, these were to:

- Comply with every general custom that does not hinder the attainment of our purpose.

- Indulge ourselves with pleasures only in so far as they are necessary for preserving health.

- Endeavor to obtain sufficient money or other commodities to enable us to preserve our life and health, and to follow such general customs as are consistent with our purpose.

Three hundred or so years later, we're offering pretty much the same advice:

- Figure out what matters and what doesn't.

- Invest your time and energy in the things that do.

- Pack your bags with the things that "enable you to live purposefully" and set aside those that don't.

Which just goes to prove that the more things change, the more they stay the same.

Life: The Final Frontier

Star Trek has it all wrong — it's not outer space that's the final frontier. It's inner space.

Albert Schweitzer wrote, "Every start upon an untrodden path is a venture which only in unusual circumstances looks sensible and likely to succeed."

Frontiers are the places we can get lost, the places we haven't yet boxed in with fences or straight roads. They are the places that once were a continent wide. Or even wider — as wide as our imaginations.

Frontiers symbolize not just new places, but also the full experience of those places. One of the real pleasures of traveling untrodden paths is the sense of freedom and independence such travel provides. Ever notice how more outgoing you are when you're in a new town that you know you'll never live in? Since nobody knows you, you can be whoever you want — or whoever you really are.

As humans, we're natural explorers. We require new challenges to sustain us. The benefits of frontiers, therefore, are not only symbolic, but practical, too. They sustain our beings and our bodies; they nourish us in our search for wholeness, and for holiness.

Like Denys Finch-Hatten, our friend Richard "Rocky" Kimball feels that a safari is not just a safari, but a spiritual and moral quest — a holy necessity. As Rocky puts it, "When our lives are at stake, we form bonds that we have at no other time. On a wilderness trek, everything is simpler, cleaner, more profound."

Rocky explains why he and Richard jumped at the chance to explore new frontiers on a safari into the center of Tanzania. "Neither of us could stay off the open roads for long. I guess we both like dust! Out there, learning is more real than in the hotel conference rooms where we often teach seminars together."

As poet and philosopher Wendell Berry says, "Solutions have perhaps the most furtive habits of any creatures; they reveal themselves very hesitantly in artificial light, and never enter air-conditioned rooms."

Experiencing Experience

The more people we talk to, the clearer it becomes to us that we're a nation of transients. Americans average eleven moves in a lifetime. Every year, an estimated 43 million of us — one-fifth of the population — move somewhere new. Given how often we relocate, you might get the impression it's something we look forward to with anticipation and joy.

Actually, for most of us, it's just the opposite.

Geographic moves are life's third-most-stressful event — right after the death of a loved one and divorce. A big part of that stress is because we tend to spend the entire experience out in front of ourselves. We rush along, out of breath, scrambling to reach a new destination where maybe, just maybe, there will be some kind of payoff — maybe the good life we've been chasing.

And yet ironically, most of us would prefer to appreciate the trip. We'd like to experience the journey with our senses wide open. But for some reason, it usually doesn't work that way. Most people don't enjoy the process — whether it's a move across the country or a move across town. All the effort put into it isn't worth the payoff. It's too little return for far too much invested.

People who have mastered the art of traveling, though, realize that it isn't about putting something in to get something out. It's about an ongoing process in which the effort and the payoff are one. If we live only for the destination, for some hoped-for success in a far-off future, we're going to totally miss the trip.

Richard admits he knows all about that.

"I Think I Missed the Trip!"

A number of years ago, I was giving a speech to an insurance industry group in Maui. I noticed a lot of T-shirts in the audience that read,

"I Survived the Road to Hana." I asked some people about it and they related tales of how incredibly beautiful it was, with its Seven Sacred Pools, its opportunities for whale-watching, and — of interest to me as a Minnesotan — the grave of Charles Lindbergh there on the tip of Maui.

I had a few hours after my speech before my flight, so after checking a map to assure myself I had time to make it, I pointed my rental car toward Hana and began driving. Thirteen switchbacks into the fifty-four that make up the "road to hell," I pulled over, opened the car door, and threw-up.

I hadn't just not survived the road to Hana, I hadn't even come close! Turning around and heading for the airport though, I resolved I'd be back.

I told the story of Hana to my then 15-year-old daughter, Greta, and she was equally excited by the prospect of visiting there one day. About a year and a half later the opportunity presented itself. This time it was a vacation in Hawaii with Greta. We added two extra days to the trip so we could include Maui and Hana. All the while over on the plane, we talked about how great it was going to be — the Seven Sacred Pools, the whales, the adventure of surviving the road to Hana.

Finally, the day arrived. We went all-out and rented a convertible. With great anticipation we set off. I told Greta we were in for the adventure of our lives — and it wouldn't even take that long. We'd be home in time to spend the afternoon at the beach so she could work on her tan.

At the sixth switchback on the road to Hana, it started raining. We put the convertible top up and discovered the rental car had no air-conditioning. This made speed imperative — both to get some airflow going and to get out of the hot, sticky car as quickly as possible.

At the twenty-fifth switchback, Greta implored me to stop. "I'm sick," she cried. "Why are we doing this? I could be at the beach!"

I assured her that she was going to love Hana, that it wasn't much farther, and promised to drive as quickly as possible the last leg of the way. I punched the accelerator as far to the floor as I could.

Finally, we entered Hana — tired, hungry, and cranky. But all we could find to refresh ourselves was an old clapboard Chinese store. We pulled into the parking lot alongside other Hana "survivors," and discovered to boot, that there were no restrooms in the vicinity. Greta and I looked at each other in silence. Meanwhile, we overheard the animated conversations of other travelers: "Did you see those whales breaching?" "Yes, but how about those botanical gardens? They were out of this world!" "Definitely, but I've never seen such beautiful trails and vistas!"

A long moment. Finally, Greta turned to me and broke the tension. "Dad," she said, "I think we missed the trip."

After a brief tour around Hana, which looked pretty much like every other small, beautiful Hawaiian town, we returned slowly, with our convertible top down, back to the beach. The drive was wonderful. We realized that on the road to Hana, it's not Hana that you're going for, it's "the road." It's not the final destination, it's the trip itself.

Greta's statement, "I think we missed the trip," has proved to be a powerful metaphor to describe the way many people live their lives. We use it all the time in speeches, conversations, and seminars — and people seem to know what we're talking about right away. We encourage them — as we encourage you now — to take the rest of the journey more like Richard and Greta did on their return — with the top down. Don't just survive the trip, live it! Enjoy the experience along the way.

Lightening Your Load

We have heard from hundreds of readers of *Repacking*. And many have told us the same thing: after finishing the book, the first thing they did was to tear through their closets and throw away all kinds of stuff they no longer needed. Old clothes, unused exercise equipment, dusty books and records, all went to the trash heap or Goodwill box.

There's something incredibly liberating about purging ourselves of unnecessary accumulation. It's like a great big sigh of relief to walk through that emptied attic or cleared-out basement. We shake our heads and wonder what in the world we were holding onto that stuff for anyway, and ask why we waited so long to get rid of it all in the first place.

But, of course, there's more to repacking than merely cleaning out our closets; and there's more to lightening our loads than merely getting rid of material possessions we no longer want. But what is it? And how can we undertake it so as to experience the profound changes so many repackers have reported?

Perhaps the most important thing we've learned in the seventeen years since *Repacking* first came out is that the act of repacking is ultimately purposeful. By this we mean that it is an act which is grounded in our appreciation of something larger than ourselves. Repacking entails wondering about what *really matters* to us and that can only be done by placing ourselves in a context that includes more than just our own individual experience.

Now, this doesn't mean that we have to align ourselves with a religious organization or go see a guru to authentically repack. It does mean, though, that we have to ask the big questions about what really matters and why.

The great challenge here is that no one can do it for us. There's no off-the-shelf ready-to-wear pre-formatted kit; to really lighten our load requires that we live in our own big questions.

And it's easy enough to think we already have the answers when we still have a long way to go.

Dave recalls the following:

> I remember soon after the original version of *Repacking* came out. I was feeling very proud of myself — being a published author finally and all — and fairly certain that I knew all about what lightening one's load was all about. One day, I was on my way to a business meeting with a prospective client. His office wasn't far from my house, so I was riding my bike. In my pannier, I had my laptop computer, an extra shirt, a mobile phone, and a loaf of bread. I remember thinking, "This is all I need in the world. This is the essence of repacking. If I could get rid of everything else and just keep what I have with me right now, that would be perfect."
>
> That, of course, was true, until it began to rain. Hard. And that's right when I began wishing I had more in my pannier — a rain jacket, for one, something warm to drink, a change of shoes and socks. I arrived at my business meeting soaked to the skin. Fortunately, my prospective client was a friend, so he didn't complain too much when I dripped all over his sofa. (I didn't, however, get any work from him.)

Riding home in the rain, I looked forward to my warm house, dry clothes, and a cup of hot coffee, all of which were waiting for me upon my arrival. Not only that, but I got plenty of sympathy and affection from my wife, Jennifer, who handed me a nice fluffy towel to dry my dripping hair, too.

As I curled up in my easy chair with my steaming cup of java, it occurred to me that I needed *more* than just my bike and the few things I was carrying on the ride. I was glad I had a home, someone who cared for me, and various creature comforts that made life good. Lightening the load was one thing; eliminating everything just for the sake of simplicity was another.

It Isn't What We Have, It's How We Have It

The question then remains: "How much (or how little) is enough?" How do we figure out what we really need? What does lightening your load really feel like?

The answer is: we all know. Every one of us has had the experience of having all that we need and no more, that feeling of being truly satisfied in the world. It's beside the point whether that's in a tent, eating freeze-dried macaroni at the end of a long day's hike, or in a luxury hotel, having a 5-course room-service dinner after lounging around the pool all afternoon. It isn't *what* we have, it's *how* we have it. The challenge is to match our values with our stuff, so that what we have is what we want — both literally and figuratively.

Many spiritual traditions teach us that the key to spiritual enlightenment is overcoming our attachments. We believe that a similar sort of worldly enlightenment follows not from eliminating our wants, but from coming to understand them in terms of their usefulness to our life's purpose. As we've said many times, some of what we're carrying *is* helping us get where we want to in life; other stuff is just weighing us down. Many of our wants are necessary to our happiness; others — often manufactured and revved up by the media and advertising — actually *prevent* us from being happy. So, we advocate learning to want what we have as opposed to being buffeted about by random desires. It makes sense to want a rain jacket if there's a risk it's going to pour, but not so much to desire a huge umbrella if there's not a cloud in the sky.

In philosophies as different as that of the ancient Greek Aristotle and the Indian sage Patanjali, we find emphasis on the personal characteristic of temperance or continence. This is the virtue or practice that has to do with regulation of the appetites. Very broadly, what is advocated isn't self-denial, but rather, a healthy appetite for life. Aristotle, for instance, encourages us to enjoy the pleasures of food, drink, and sexuality; however, we are admonished to do so in the right way at the right time, as the virtuous person would.

This is consistent with our message here. Lightening one's load doesn't entail fasting and asceticism; rather, it's a matter of wanting and having the right amount at the right time in the right way and for the right reasons. It's not about eliminating desires; it's about learning not to be controlled by them. It isn't what we have; it's how we have it.

Back to the Rhythm

"That's it." Daudi Peterson points out ahead to Rocky and me. "The Yaida Valley. Where the Hadzas are."

For several years, Daudi and Richard had been talking about going "back to the rhythm" — to travel with the Hadzas and learn their traditional hunter-gatherer ways.

Daudi says he's long been attracted to this wild country, an area which on the map, "has yet to be divided into straight lines." And he's right. Less than half a mile from the road, the last signs of civilization abruptly ends. Africa — the real Africa — begins, which means endless thornbush, rough tracks, and in this case, a steep descent into the Yaida Valley.

And an even steeper descent back to the rhythm.

As we make our way off the edge of a changing world, into a rugged, prehistoric-looking landscape, we literally feel as if we are dropping back into the past.

The earliest inhabitants of Tanzania were hunter-gatherers that occupied the area at least 70,000 years ago. Some of their shelters, stone tools, and weapons have survived. So have the Hadza, who are thought to be remnants of those early people.

"Where's the coke bottle?"

Rocky has whispered to me the exact same words — a reference to the film *The Gods Must Be Crazy* — that were going through my head. This place, and the people we are meeting, all look straight out of a *Discovery Channel* documentary on our hunter-gatherer ancestors.

Our three Hadza guides are wearing cloth that matches the color of the parched ground on which they stand. Each carries a bow that's about the same size as he is, but he also speaks with an intensity that seems at least as dangerous as the poison arrows in his quiver.

Perhaps because of their relative isolation and resistance to outsiders, the Hadza have developed a substantial degree of self-consciousness. As shy as they seem, they are genuinely pleased to welcome us to their village and to show us the old ways of hunting and gathering.

In a "blinding glimpse of the obvious," I realize that this is not going to be your typical vacation. A vacation, according to the dictionary, is a "respite from something." This, on the other hand, is a journey into something — what Rocky calls the "Land of I Don't Know." It's a rare opportunity to venture down untrodden paths, to get out from under the safety net of interpreted experience. It's an opportunity, I realize, that I've really been hungering for.

Rocky says that when he crosses from the "Land of I Know" into the "Land of I Don't Know" that he has to attain a beginner's mind, to be non-judgmental, and to go into situations admitting that he knows nothing at all. He tries to see the people around him as neither strange nor foreign, but simply as people — his own people.

It takes us no more than an hour to cross completely into the "Land of I Don't Know" and to get back to the rhythm I was seeking — where schedules are forgotten and experience feels pure.

We follow behind the Hadza guides as they move silently through the bush, vanishing and then, like apparitions, suddenly reappearing. To see them stalking is a revelation. Here are the original hunter-gatherers, completely in tune with their natural environment. So light are their movements that a dry twig rarely cracks under their feet. Thorns hardly delay them, and when Rocky, Daudi, and I become hopelessly entangled in these "wait-a-bit" bushes, our guides remove them with swift gentleness before the barbs can hook us deeply.

Suddenly, the smallest man, Maroba, stops and stares at a huge baobab tree twenty yards away. We hear the whistle of a birdsong and Maroba whistles back. He points to a small gray bird, about the size of a robin, fluttering from branch to branch.

"He wants to show us the honey, the sweet honey that we like so much," says Maroba. "He is the Honey Guide — a friend of the Hadza."

For the next half hour, we hurry after the bird as it flies from tree to tree, leading us on. At intervals, it stops and waits, anxious as a dog for its master, whistling for us to hurry. And Maroba, his face filled with joy, whistles back.

Finally, the bird alights on a large acacia tree, to which it directs us with a joyous, anticipatory song. Maroba surveys the tree for a brief moment and quickly locates the beehive in it. He collects a dry clump of grass and sets it on fire by spinning a fire-stick between his hands. Once the fire has taken, he grasps the burning clump and plunges it into a hole in the tree to smoke out the bees.

I'm mesmerized by how he avoids getting stung. Time and again he carefully reaches into the hole — all the way up to his shoulder — and pulls out handfuls of honeycomb, wax, and larvae. The first few batches he shovels into his mouth. The rest he shares with his companions and us, leaving an ample portion for the Honey Guide patiently waiting its turn in the tree above.

Throughout the morning the same scenario repeats itself over and over. New Honey Guides suddenly appear to lead us on another wild treasure hunt. But later, in the growing heat of the African sun, our three Hadza hosts seem to lose their way. One or another of them is constantly zig-zagging away, apparently off to check for landmarks of some sort. I'm amazed that they can find their way back to us, much less out of the bush, and I'm thinking that if they're lost, then we're really lost, and it's going to take a lot more than a Honey Guide to show us the way home.

To make matters worse, we're all getting pretty thirsty. Nothing like a breakfast of honey and bee larvae to parch the palate. And as far as Rocky, Daudi, and I can tell, this land is as dry as we are. But the Hadza assure us that there is a river nearby that, even during the current drought, will have water.

Just as I'm starting to wish for a "Water Guide" to show up, the Hadza lead us down to the river — several pools of water in the blistering hot sand which appear to have been the watering holes for a herd of zebra the night before. How they found this little oasis is beyond me, but I'm too busy refreshing myself to ask questions.

Rocky, losing steam from heat and the effects of too many helpings of bee pollen and larvae, crashes in the shade of a some trees on the river bank.

The Secret of Life

In retrospect, Richard realized that with the Hadza, they were never lost. Which is to say, they always were. But unlike most of us, the Hadza knew how to stand still and listen. To let the trees find them. In their willingness to treat the unknown as a powerful stranger and welcome it into their lives, they demonstrated their understanding of the real secret of life:

Presence is everything.

The Hadza knew how to simultaneously make life happen and let life happen. No matter what they did, they did it with their whole selves — fully present in the moment. Moving joyfully through the harsh environment in a state of flow, they focused on one thing and only one thing at a time. But in doing so, the whole world opened up to them.

Richard recalls what that felt like:

Never have I traveled with so little, yet never have I felt so secure, so alive. Most of the time, I trek with enough to cover all the contingencies; this time, we just walked off into the bush and started living. At times, I feel that my life has not yet started — that I'm waiting for just the right time to really begin. With the Hadza, I realized that unless, like Maroba, I can learn to see everything as if it were for the first time, the future will always be a disappointment.

Simply Finding Yourself

When the Hadza "lost" their trail in the forest, they didn't panic. They didn't engage in a lot of frantic activity trying to figure out where they were and where to go next. Instead, they engaged their senses. They listened. They looked. They let themselves experience the experience.

In today's radically changing world, we all feel lost from time to time — or perhaps, most of the time. We keep trying to retrace our steps back to a place that feels familiar, a place to gather our bearings, but those places are gone forever. More than ever before, being lost is a familiar place. So we need to find a way, like the Hadza, to turn that experience into a way of finding ourselves.

It takes courage and acceptance — courage to face the new, and acceptance of one's need to learn. It's the difference between the attitude of a tourist and an adventurer. The tourist merely visits life, checking sites off a list. The adventurer experiences life, immersing head and heart in the totality of it. Ultimately, the difference has to do with a willingness to get lost.

An entry from Richard's Africa journal the evening after his day with the Hadza makes it clear.

> Being lost in Africa is incredibly important to me. I experience so much about myself — not all of it pleasant — and that's the stuff I need to keep in touch with. This last year I've spent more time promoting living than I did living. Here today, I realize that I'm tired of trying to promote a sense of hope and living up to others' image of me. Today, I was not explaining life, but living it. And it felt great.
>
> I'm happiest, it seems, out here where life is least complex. Where life is the simplest, I realize all that matters is love — relationships I have with Andy, Greta, Sally, and those around me, a sense of place — being connected to the earth, and work — doing work that I love. Beyond that, everything is simply maintenance.

"Why Must Success Weigh So Much?"

"Jambo Richard! Habari gani?"

Koyie greets me in Swahili, asking for the news. We are standing in the center of his kraal, surrounded by about a hundred noisy animals — cows, donkeys, and goats. Koyie looks right at home, but I am shifting around nervously. I feel crowded by the animals and their smell, even in the cool evening air, is overpowering.

Koyie's life revolves around his animals. It's understandable, since they provide most of what he needs to subsist. Their milk is part of his daily fare; their skin a basic material for clothing; their blood may be used as an emergency ration. Even their dung is used for fuel and building — nothing is wasted.

Koyie and I stand in the semi-darkness discussing cattle. He tells me of the intimate bond that exists between his animals and himself. He knows each of his cattle by voice, by color, and by the names he has for them all.

Two of Koyie's children arrive, lowering their heads for the touch of my hand in greeting. I am deferred to as a *mzee* — an elder — an honor which, I comfort myself, is accorded to persons older than thirty.

Koyie leads me toward the *boma* of the first of his three wives. Its outer appearance resembles a long oval loaf of brown bread. The curved entrance is a dark tunnel to prevent rain and flies from finding their way into the cool, smoky-smelling living area.

In a small hearth made of three stones, two one-inch sticks are burning, providing a constant light and temperature. On either side are two sleeping coves, neatly crafted with tightly woven sticks covered by bare skins. One cove is for husband and wife, the other for children or guests.

Koyie's wife, a small woman with large, bright eyes and delicate features, greets me in a soft voice. She continues to breastfeed her child while stirring a fresh batch of honey beer.

Honey beer is the traditional Maasai drink for elders and guests at ritual ceremonies. It may take up to three weeks to make. The golden liquid is prepared in a large, round calabash and placed near the fire to ferment under the careful attention of a skilled brewmaster like Koyie's wife.

Standing there, I am struck by the apparent perfection of the scene. It seems to me that here, in this simple *boma,* Koyie has it all — a sense of place, love, meaningful work, and a purpose.

Though his world is small, Koyie's concerns are large. Even now, he is deeply involved in shaping the future of his people and their fight for their own version of the good life. A true visionary, Koyie can see the coming challenges. The Maasai, like people everywhere, are in the midst of radical change — change where the young are moving away from their elders, impatient to discover what the modern world has to offer. So I am doubly impressed by his ability to maintain a sense of quiet calm amidst the building storm.

Offering me a honey beer, Koyie asks, "So Richard, what kind of good life are these people traveling with you seeking? The more people you bring to my village, the clearer it becomes that most are seeking something. At the start of your treks, all these people, all these successful people, seem to be struggling with some heavy weight. So I ask you, why must success weigh so much?"

I answer that I think all these people are searching for their own vision of the good life. Then, I ask him what he thinks. He sets down his honey beer and picks up the new journal and pen that I have brought him as a gift. He writes quickly but neatly, in careful strokes. He shows me what he has written, in Maa, the Maasai language:

Meetay oidpa, oitumura ake-etay

"It's an old Maasai saying, a definition of the good life," explains Koyie. "It means something like living passionately for today and purposefully for tomorrow. It means you can only enjoy now, no matter how rich you are. It all comes to an end soon."

He keeps trying to make it clearer. "It means being able to be happy today is the real proof of success. It may seem simple to you, Richard, but the good life to me means appreciating all the ways I am already a success — my health, my cattle, children, good rains. What's the use of worrying about enough milk for next week unless I can enjoy the milk now? Does that make sense?"

I sip my honey beer and reflect on how he has captured perfectly what I've been striving to say all along. But it's always like this with Koyie. When I'm with him, speaking the language haltingly, feeling like a shy student, I somehow get in touch with and reveal parts of myself that usually remain hidden to others — even to myself. I experience all the basic human vulnerabilities, feelings of incompetence, and deep-seated needs for approval. But somehow, Koyie makes me feel what I think we all know somewhere deep inside — that our true value is more than what we do, how much we make, or how many things we own — it's simply who we are.

"So Richard, what do you think? The best I can offer you and your friends is to live passionately for today and purposefully for tomorrow. Does that help?"

That evening, after I leave Koyie, his words and image remain in my mind, and they hearten me, rekindling my faith in human nature. I see the picture of Koyie, the Maasai elder, his blanket around him, gazing at the fire, and off toward the infinite horizon. Koyie has lightened his load by living passionately for today and purposefully for tomorrow.

Learning to pack and repack our bags — is a central lesson of our time. But it is a lesson we all can learn by living passionately for today and purposefully for tomorrow, and in doing so, lighten our load to live the good life.

The Good Life Inventory

To find out how well your current version of the good life fits your desired vision of "living in the place I call home, with the people I love, doing the right work, on purpose," rate each question by numbering one to seven, with seven being best. For each question, write a score from one to seven, based on how well it fits your vision of the good life.

A second column is provided for use with a Repacking Partner. Have your partner fill out that column — rating you — and then discuss the results afterwards. Or, to make it even more interesting, make a copy of the Inventory, and give it to your partner. Each of you can then complete both columns, rating yourselves and each other. That discussion afterwards promises to be twice as compelling.

KEY CHARACTERISTICS OF THE GOOD LIFE	YOUR SCORE	PARTNER'S SCORE
UNPACKING		
1. I'm living my own version of the Good Life.		
2. I regularly say "no" to the less important things in my life and "yes" to my real priorities.		
3. I keep the small promises I make to myself.		
4. I go to sleep most nights feeling that "this was a well-lived day."		
5. I have a regular time and place — a "listening point" — to renew myself.		
PLACE		
6. I'm living in my ideal place.		
7. I feel at home in my home.		
8. I feel like I belong in my community.		
9. I have options in the place that I live to do the things I love to do.		
10. My place makes me happy.		
PEOPLE		
11. I have at least one person who truly listens to me, with whom I can "fully unpack my bags."		
12. I regularly have "courageous conversations" with people.		
13. I share my life dreams with the people I'm closest to.		
14. I'm spending the right amount of time with my friends and loved ones.		
15. My relationships make me happy.		

KEY CHARACTERISTICS OF THE GOOD LIFE	YOUR SCORE	PARTNER'S SCORE
WORK		
16. I am doing work that fully engages my true gifts.		
17. I am using my gifts in support of something I am passionate about.		
18. I am in a work environment that is nutritious for me.		
19. I receive rewards that matter to me.		
20. My work makes me happy.		
PURPOSE		
21. I have a clear reason to get up in the morning.		
22. I have a healthy spiritual life.		
23. I live a lifestyle which supports positive kinship with the natural world.		
24. My work serves the world in some distinct way.		
25. My purpose makes me happy.		
REPACKING		
26. I have defined how much is enough money for me.		
27. I'm satisfied with how my time and money are being spent.		
28. I know where I'm headed on life's journey.		
29. I have uncovered my calling.		
30. My life makes me happy.		
TOTALS		

Scoring

180+:   Your life fits your definition of the good life. Enjoy your good fortune and assist others in attaining a similar quality of life.

150-180:   Parts of the Good Life formula are missing. Explore ways to "keep the small promises you've made to yourself."

120-150:   Your current life/work is adequate, based on your vision of the good life. But what's up ahead?

90-120:   Your current life/work does not fit your vision of the good life. Choose your timetable and set priorities for making changes.

Under 90:   Your life/work is a poor fit for your vision of the good life. It looks like it's time for "courageous conversations" and choice. Now!

Having completed this exercise, sit quietly for a few moments and reflect on your Good Life Inventory. Take a look at your life. What do you want? How will you know when you get it? Are you living in the Place you belong? Are you living with the People you love? Are you doing the right Work? Are you living and working On Purpose? What do you need to "unpack" to live the Good Life? What do you need to "repack"?

The Good Life Checklist

As you went through *The Good Life Inventory*, what you were doing, essentially, was creating a customized trip checklist, or what we call *The Good Life Checklist*.

The Good Life Checklist is simply a way to make sure that you're bringing the essentials with you on your journey. And at the same time, not bringing way too much. A way to avoid the "Packing Principle."

You're taking stock of where you are and how you've gotten here. You're examining the choices you've made in your life and trying to determine if the decisions still serve you. You're seeing if you still have the answers . . . or if even the questions have changed.

The Good Life Checklist is a tool to eventually help you decide what you'll need to carry on the next part of your journey. It's designed to help you identify what you're carrying (and what you're not) and what you really need for the trip ahead.

The Good Life Checklist isn't a test. Think of it more as a resource for planning. There are no right or wrong answers. The point is simply answer as truthfully as possible and learn as much about yourself as you possibly can.

Use *The Good Life Checklist* below to take a look at the next phase of your life. See if you're carrying these items, or if some of the other things you're lugging are taking up all of the room.

THE GOOD LIFE CHECKLIST

CHECKLIST ITEM	HAVE IT	NEED IT
Passport		
Where am I going?		
Why am I going there?		
Baggage		
What am I carrying?		
Why am I carrying it?		
Map		
What's my vision for where I'll end up?		
What side trips will I take along the way?		
Money		
Do I have the cash I need?		
Do I have credit cards just in case?		
Address Book		
Who are my travel advisors?		
Who are my travel partners?		
Itinerary		
What if I get lost?		
What if I don't get lost?		
Adventuring Spirit		
What do I need to unpack and let go of?		
What do I need to repack and hold onto?		

The Good Life Checklist Check-In

Having completed *The Good Life Checklist,* you may be asking yourself, "What do I really need to get where I'm going, anyway?"

The Good Life Checklist provides you with a structure for discussing what you're carrying (and what else you may need) with others.

Courageous Conversation is an important part of *The Good life Checklist.*

Use the checklist in a discussion with a Repacking Partner to explore questions like:

- What type of bag (backpack, attaché case, duffel bag, etc.) best illustrates where I am and where I'm going next?

- What are my hopes and fears for the next leg of my journey?

- What is preventing me from getting where I'm going and what is weighing me down?

- Who are my current travel partners and who else might I seek out?

Keep the dialogue open and alive with a willingness to share as deeply as feels comfortable. Remember, this is about unpacking and repacking. The more fully you can unpack your innermost thoughts and feelings, the more vital your discussions will turn out to be.

At the same time there's no need to turn your conversations into therapy sessions. They should be fun — or at least not *too* painful. Like your life, they should be filled with all the stuff you need, and free from all the stuff you don't.

Each of our lives is, in fact, a short trip. In the grand scheme of things, we're penciled in for a very brief journey. On the other hand, this is all we've got. So it's no surprise that many of us go through life weighed down by the importance of it all, crushed beneath our load of literal and figurative baggage.

You can gain insight into how to lighten your load by imagining yourself setting out on a journey into the wilderness. If your pack is too heavy, it means you're too attached to the life you are leaving behind. If it's too light, it means you may not have enough to stay alive. The question becomes "How much is enough?" The weight of your pack ultimately determines the quality of your trip.

Since the more we have, the more we have to carry, entering the next phase of our trip requires lightening our load — not just physically but also emotionally. Like trekkers on safari, we inevitably have to ask, "What do I really need to carry?"

In the middle stages of a trek people often get tired because they're carrying too much. They lose their sense of joy because they're weighed down by all their stuff. They experience a version of the distinction that comedian George Carlin draws so eloquently between our "stuff" and other people's "stuff." In his routine, "A Place for My Stuff," our own stuff is "stuff," while other people's stuff is "shit." During a trek people often come to believe that their own stuff is shit, too.

To many of us during different stages of life, carrying our baggage starts to feel like an all-or-nothing choice. We get buried in responsibilities and attachments, and want to either chuck them all or just give up. Often this is what's behind the traditional midlife crisis that sports car dealers know so well.

On treks in Africa most people don't have a problem knowing what to carry. Their problem is knowing what to leave behind.

The trick is to find the balance between what to carry and what to leave — so you have all you need, but need all you have.

Creating a Repacking Group

It is not necessary to go it alone.

We were not destined to struggle all by ourselves, even if at the core of our lives we have to find our own way. It can be very reassuring and quite motivating to see others engaged in the same explorations as your own. Listening to and sharing with people that are similarly discovering what it means to repack can make the process seem more real and more accessible. In a variety of ways, people in this kind of supportive group feed off one another's energy, enthusiasm, stories, and insight. All benefit as a result.

A Repacking Group inspires us to clarify our own vision of the good life, and to live it as fully as possible. Doing so reduces the likelihood that we will meander through life and end up regretting choices we made or failed to make. Having a group to rely on connects us to others who share our interests and acts as an antidote to social isolation.

The Repacking Group challenges us to discover the feeling of aliveness — the belief that "I'm on course." It releases the power underlying a sense of purpose and vision.

Even though reading the book can be a powerful growth experience in itself, the presence of other individuals in a group setting will lend strength and breadth to the content. Your group can be a real source of inspiration, mutual support, and the formation of lasting friendships. So many individuals are searching for "what's next?" in their lives that it could even be the beginning of a growth-support network in your region.

The following discussion section is your guide for leading a group exploration into the issues surrounding unpacking, repacking, and living the good life.

Using selections from the text of *Repacking Your Bags,* and with the help of a facilitator, a Repacking group can offer the opportunity for us to reflect on our lives. The meetings can be held at someone's home on an evening or for four weekly (or monthly) meetings.

Each Repacking group is an organic entity with a personality and intelligence all its own. The guidelines here are offered as a basic structure upon which you can build. Starting a Repacking group can provide a fun way to begin and sustain the process of taking creative control of your life, while helping others to do the same.

Membership

The ideal size for a lively discussion is around six to eight people, assuming that it is a participative group. When deciding how many people to include in your group, however, you must take into account other factors, such as busy schedules, that can often keep several people from attending. The best strategy is to have enough people join the group so that you are assured of six to eight participants at the meeting(s).

You are advised to restrict membership to those who are seriously committed to the Repacking process. It undermines the energy of the group to allow dabblers at your sessions, for example, group members' spouses or partners who are not themselves seeking a new experience of repacking.

Group members should be expected to attend all sessions, to complete readings and inventories, and to fully participate in group discussions. Each participant should have a copy of *Repacking Your Bags*.

Leadership

Without clear direction and a well-focused agenda your Repacking gatherings run the risk of degenerating into chat, gossip, or gripe sessions in which energy and time are expended but little is accomplished. In order to avoid this we strongly suggest that your group designates a facilitator for the session(s). It will be the facilitator's responsibility to set the meeting agenda and to keep the group focused and moving forward.

The role of the facilitator is to keep people on track, to make certain that there is a positive dialogue maintained throughout, and that the group does not get involved in personal problem-solving or therapy. This does not mean that the input of individuals is not welcome. Actually it is essential, but the primary goal is the personal understanding and application of the exercises and discussion. The facilitator is not a guru, but rather a fellow participant and explorer.

Before facilitating the Repacking group, take the following steps:

1. Read *Repacking Your Bags*.

2. Complete *The Good Life Inventory*.

3. Let the material digest mentally for a day or two. Think about interesting information that would highlight the process.

4. Look over *Repacking* again and make notes. Prepare your own stimulating questions and insightful examples. Personal stories and anecdotes will often trigger discussions.

How Often Should You Meet?

The group format is totally flexible. It can be used in a short, two-hour session or a longer four-week or four-month format. It can be used in a coaching relationship or as part of a class or study group. If you are using the group process over time it is a good idea to meet on some predictable day, such as the first Wednesday of each month.

Where Should You Meet?

You could meet in a participant's home or rotate among participants' homes. You could use library rooms, local community centers, conference rooms, churches, synagogues, temples, spas and health clubs. Of course, conference calls or online discussions are a possibility for some types of groups.

Check that the site meets these criteria:

- Informal atmosphere

- Large enough to hold the maximum number of people expected

- Area is well-lit and temperature controlled

- Refreshments are available (or can be brought in)

What Are the Participant's Responsibilities?

Again, each participant should have a copy of *Repacking*. Each should also bring a notebook or journal and a pen. The most obvious responsibility of participants is to read the book and complete *The Good Life Inventory* before the meeting. Other ground rules should be discussed at the initial meeting. The discussion might include issues of punctuality; what time meetings will begin and end; expectations of group members regarding level and consistency of participation; what happens if participants need to miss a session; and whether or not guests are allowed.

Structure

The facilitator is responsible for:

- Monitoring start and stop times.

- Encouraging dialogue from all participants.

- Reviewing the book and booklets carefully for specific discussion topics.

- Answering the following questions:
  - Where will we meet?
  - When will we meet?
  - How will we notify people of meeting locations, times and study selections?
  - How will we purchase the materials; individually or as a group?

Although there is a tendency with some facilitators to teach or preach, the *Repacking* lends itself to full group participation. When people participate they enjoy themselves more, and tend to get more out of the experience. Here are a few simple steps that will help you encourage group participation:

1. Practice good communication skills. Use eye contact and first names.

2. Ask open-ended questions that cannot be answered with a simple "yes" or "no." For instance, "What are your thoughts about this?" or "How do you feel about that?" Ask for examples from the group's experience.

3. Wait for a response. Don't feel that you always have to fill silence. If you wait, the participants will take the initiative.

4. Get everyone to participate. Direct questions to people holding back. Use a "mood check" (go around) technique to begin.

5. Cut long-winded speakers. Redirect statements made to you as the facilitator. Turn away from the speaker and ask another participant to reply. Turn questions back to the group.

6. Keep on target and to the point. Don't stray to unrelated subjects and don't concentrate on small points for too long.

7. Give recognition. If you are impressed by a participant's remark or insight, say so.

8. Keep your personal assessments hidden until several points of view have been aired and understood.

9. Show enjoyment of the group. Spend additional time with people before and after sessions and during the breaks.

10. Take frequent breaks so that individuals have time to communicate privately. Break the group up into pairs or triads for several of the exercises, and vary who is talking to whom. Smaller groups help to create a feeling of comfort and reduce anxiety. At the beginning it is also helpful to permit participants to talk a bit about themselves and what they are looking for out of the experience.

Guidelines

We are suggesting two different program structures to give you optional courses of action and to help you design your own program. You will probably want to make changes to complement the composition and objectives of your group, as well as your time requirements.

Option 1: One Session, two hours in length

Option 2: Four Sessions, two hours each

(same process as Option 1 but allowing more time)

Process

1. As soon as participants enter the room, try to develop rapport. Introduce yourself. If the group does not know each other, have them pick up a name tag as they walk in.

2. When everyone is in place and ready to begin, summarize the "Repacking" concept in your own words.

3. Ask starter questions to stimulate thinking and discussion. Do not feel obliged to pose the questions word for word. Use them instead to help you define, enhance and organize your own facilitation process.

    a. What are some clear examples of repacking that you can recall? In your life? In your family? With people you know?

    b. What is the role of repacking in life? Why is repacking necessary? When is it not necessary?

    c. Review and share each others' *Good Life Inventory.*

    d. When do your feelings of living the good life typically emerge? When are they submerged?

    e. How might we find a sense of purpose at this stage of your life?

    f. Are you "living in the place you belong, with people you love, doing the right work, on purpose"? If not, which component(s) are lacking?

4. Have each member of the group share a Repacking story. What's working and what isn't? What support would help?

5. You can conclude with a "mood check." Ask each person to share their insights and takeaways from the session.

Repacking Resources

The Good Life

Choosing the Right Thing to Do, David A. Shapiro, Berrett-Koehler, 1999.

Something to Live For: Finding Your Way in the Second Half of Life, Richard J. Leider and David A. Shapiro, Berrett-Koehler, 2008.

Spontaneous Happiness, Andrew Weil, Little-Brown, 2011.

Living in the Place You Belong...

When All You Ever Wanted Isn't Enough, Harold Kushner, Summit 1986.

Transitions: Making Sense of Life's Changes, William Bridges, Addison-Wesley, 1980.

Walden, Henry David Thoreau (many versions).

Holding the Center: Sanctuary in a Time of Confusion, Richard Strozzi-Heckler, Frog Books, 1997.

With the People You Love...

True North Groups, Bill George and Doug Baker, Berrett-Koehler, 2011.

The Way of Transition, William Bridges, Perseus, 2001.

Composing a Further Life, Mary Catherine Bateson, Plume, 1990.

When Things Fall Apart: Heart Advice for Difficult Times, Pema Chodron, Shambhala, 2005.

I Will Not Die An Unlived Life, Dawna Markova, Conari Press, 2000.

Doing the Right Work . . .

Whistle While You Work, Richard J. Leider and David A. Shapiro, Berrett-Koehler, 2001.

What Color is Your Parachute? Richard Bolles, Ten Speed Press, 2012.

Let Your Life Speak, Parker Palmer, Jossey-Bass, 1999.

On Purpose

The Power of Purpose, Richard J. Leider, Berrett-Koehler, 2010.

Timeshifting: Creating Time to Enjoy Your Life, Stephan Rechtschaffen, MD, Doubleday, 1996.

Man's Search for Meaning, Viktor Frankl, Pocket Books, 1963

Claiming Your Place at the Fire, Richard J. Leider and David A. Shapiro, Berrett-Koehler, 2004.

Notes

1. May, Rollo, *The Courage to Create,* New York: Norton, 1975.

2. Olson, Sigurd, *Listening Point,* New York: Knopf, 1958.

3. Nearing, Helen, *Loving and Leaving the Good Life,* White River Junction, VT: Chelsea Green Publishing, 1992.

4. Olson, Sigurd, *Listening Point,* New York: Knopf, 1958.

5. Thoreau, Henry David, *Walden*, in *Walden and Civil Disobedience,* New York: Penguin Books, 1985.

6. Mason, Marilyn, *Intimacy,* Hazelden: Hazelden Foundation, 1986, p.1.

7. Russell, Peter, *The White Hole in Time: Our Future Evolution and the Meaning of Now,* New York: Harper Collins, 1992, p.135.

8. Jourard, Sidney, *The Transparent Self,* New York: Van Nostrand Reinhold, 1971.

9. Vaillant, George E., *Adaptation to Life,* Boston: Little, Brown, 1977.

10. Kerr, Walter, *The Decline of Pleasure,* New York: Time Inc., 1966.

11. Bach, Richard, *Illusions: The Adventures of a Reluctant Messiah,* New York: Delecorte, 1977.

12. Russell, Peter, *The White Hole in Time: Our Future Evolution and the Meaning of Now,* New York: Harper Collins, 1992, p. 125.

13. Kubler Ross, Elisabeth, *Living With Death and Dying,* New York: Macmillan, 1981.

14. McCoy, Buzz, "The Parable of the Sadhu," in *The Harvard Business Review,* 1997.

15. Alexander, Lamar, *Six Months Off: An American Family's Australian Adventure,* New York: Morrow, 1988.

16. Elgin, Duane, *Voluntary Simplicity: Toward a Way of Life That Is Outwardly Simple and Inwardly Rich,* New York: Morrow, 1981.

17. Bolles, Richard, *The Three Boxes of Life and How To Get Out of Them,* Berkeley, CA: Ten Speed Press, 1981.

Index

About the Authors

Richard J. Leider

Richard J. Leider is a widely read and internationally recognized speaker, author, and life coach. Founder and Chairman of The Inventure Group, a coaching and consulting firm in Minneapolis, MN, Richard is consistently rated as one of the top executive educators and coaches in the world. As a speaker and seminar leader, he has taught over 100,000 executives from more than 50 corporations worldwide. He is an Executive Fellow at the University of Minnesota Carlson School of Management, and a guest lecturer in both the Harvard Business School's General Management Program and Duke Corporate Education's Global Resource Network.

Richard is the author of eight books, including three best-sellers, and his work has been translated into 21 languages. *Repacking Your Bags* and *The Power of Purpose* are considered classics in the personal development field. *Claiming Your Place at the Fire* and *Something to Live*

For have been touted as breakthrough books on "positive aging." Richard is a contributing author to many leading-edge coaching books, including *Coaching for Leadership, The Art and Practice of Leadership Coaching, Executive Coaching for Results,* and *The Organization of the Future.*

Richard holds a Master's Degree in Counseling and is a Nationally Certified Master Career Counselor. He is a Senior Fellow at the University of Minnesota's Center for Spirituality and Healing, where he is a founder of *The Purpose Project.* As a commentator on "life work" issues, Richard appears in the *Wall Street Journal, The New York Times, USA Today,* and on PBS television, NPR, and other media sources.

A pioneer and leader in the field of coaching, Richard is widely recognized for his innovative work on helping people to discover "the power of purpose." His work received recognition from the Bush Foundation, from which he was awarded a Bush Fellowship to study "purposeful aging." He was named a "Distinguished Alumnus" by Gustavus Adolphus College and was inducted to the "Hall of Fame" at Central High School in St. Paul, MN.

Along with his professional pursuits, Richard has led annual Inventure Expedition walking safaris in Tanzania, East Africa for more than 27 years.

David A. Shapiro

JEN DIXON

David A. Shapiro is a writer, philosopher, and educator who specializes in exploring questions about ethics and the good life. A fulltime faculty member at Cascadia Community College near Seattle, he is also the Education Director of the University of Washington's Northwest Center for Philosophy for Children, a non-profit organization that brings philosophy and philosophers into the lives of young people in schools and community forums.

David is the author of *Choosing the Right Thing to Do: In Life, At Work, In Relationships,* and *For the Planet, Plato Was Wrong! Footnotes on Doing Philosophy with Young People,* and co-author, along with Richard Leider, of *Whistle While You Work: Heeding Your Life's Calling, Claiming Your Place at the Fire: Living the Second Half of Your Life on Purpose,* and *Something to Live For: Finding Your Way in the Second Half of Life.*

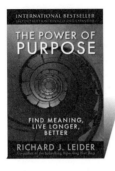

Claiming Your Place at the Fire
Living the Second Half of Your Life on Purpose

Leider and Shapiro show readers how to claim their rightful place as new elders, men and women who "use the second half of life as an empty canvas, a blank page, a hunk of clay to be crafted on purpose." They help readers address four key questions: *Who am I? Where do I belong? What do I care about? What is my purpose?*

Paperback, 168 pages, ISBN 978-1-57675-297-5
PDF ebook, ISBN 978-1-57675-877-9

Whistle While You Work
Heeding Your Life's Calling

Calling is natural. We all possess it. It needs only to be uncovered, not discovered. *Whistle While You Work* makes the uncovering process inspiring and fun. Featuring a unique "Calling Card" exercise—a powerful way to put the whistle in your work—it is a liberating and practical guide that will help you find work that is truly satisfying, deeply fulfilling, and consistent with your deepest values.

Paperback, 168 pages, ISBN 978-1-57675-103-9
PDF ebook, ISBN 978-1-57675-952-3

Berrett–Koehler Publishers, Inc.
www.bkconnection.com

800.929.2929

Berrett–Koehler
BK Publishers

Berrett-Koehler is an independent publisher dedicated to an ambitious mission: *Creating a World That Works for All*.

We believe that to truly create a better world, action is needed at all levels—individual, organizational, and societal. At the individual level, our publications help people align their lives with their values and with their aspirations for a better world. At the organizational level, our publications promote progressive leadership and management practices, socially responsible approaches to business, and humane and effective organizations. At the societal level, our publications advance social and economic justice, shared prosperity, sustainability, and new solutions to national and global issues.

A major theme of our publications is "Opening Up New Space." Berrett-Koehler titles challenge conventional thinking, introduce new ideas, and foster positive change. Their common quest is changing the underlying beliefs, mindsets, institutions, and structures that keep generating the same cycles of problems, no matter who our leaders are or what improvement programs we adopt.

We strive to practice what we preach—to operate our publishing company in line with the ideas in our books. At the core of our approach is stewardship, which we define as a deep sense of responsibility to administer the company for the benefit of all of our "stakeholder" groups: authors, customers, employees, investors, service providers, and the communities and environment around us.

We are grateful to the thousands of readers, authors, and other friends of the company who consider themselves to be part of the "BK Community." We hope that you, too, will join us in our mission.

A BK Life Book

This book is part of our BK Life series. BK Life books change people's lives. They help individuals improve their lives in ways that are beneficial for the families, organizations, communities, nations, and world in which they live and work. To find out more, visit **www.bk-life.com**.

Berrett–Koehler
Publishers

A community dedicated to creating
a world that works for all

Visit Our Website: www.bkconnection.com

Read book excerpts, see author videos and Internet movies, read our authors' blogs, join discussion groups, download book apps, find out about the BK Affiliate Network, browse subject-area libraries of books, get special discounts, and more!

Subscribe to Our Free E-Newsletter, the *BK Communiqué*

Be the first to hear about new publications, special discount offers, exclusive articles, news about bestsellers, and more! Get on the list for our free e-newsletter by going to **www.bkconnection.com**.

Get Quantity Discounts

Berrett-Koehler books are available at quantity discounts for orders of ten or more copies. Please call us toll-free at (800) 929-2929 or email us at **bkp .orders@aidcvt.com**.

Join the BK Community

BKcommunity.com is a virtual meeting place where people from around the world can engage with kindred spirits to create a world that works for all. **BKcommunity.com** members may create their own profiles, blog, start and participate in forums and discussion groups, post photos and videos, answer surveys, announce and register for upcoming events, and chat with others online in real time. Please join the conversation!